ON BECOMING

TEEN WISE

*Building a Relationship
That Lasts a Lifetime*

GARY EZZO, M.A. AND
ROBERT BUCKNAM, M.D.

PARENT-WISE SOLUTIONS
SIMI VALLEY, CALIFORNIA

ON BECOMING TEENWISE
published by Parent-Wise Solutions, Inc.

© 2000 by Gary Ezzo and Robert Bucknam, M.D.
International Standard Book Number: 0-9714532-5-X

Cover image by Tony Stone Images

Printed in the United States of America

For information:
Parent-Wise Solutions, Inc
1846 Angus Ave. Simi Valley CA 93063

Library of Congress Cataloging-in-Publication Data:
Ezzo, Gary. On becoming teenwise: building a relationship that lasts a life-
time/by Gary Ezzo and Robert Bucknam.
    p. cm.
ISBN 0-9714532-5-X
1. Teenagers—Family relationships. 2. Parent and teenager. 3. Parenting.
    4. Adolescent psychology. I. Bucknam, Robert. II. Title.
HQ799.15.E947 2000
649'.125—dc21
00-010143

01 02 03 04 05 06 — 10 9 8 7 6 5 4 3 2 1

To Michael and Diane Cadorette,
Noble Friends
A noble life enriches the men and women who live it.
We who come after are made better by their example.

TABLE OF CONTENTS

INTRODUCTION: ARE WE LOST?

There's an old *Far Side* cartoon about a husband and wife driving on the surface of the moon. The wife says, "For heaven's sake, Elroy!... NOW look where the earth is!... Move over and let me drive!"

Parents of teenagers can feel like that: so utterly off the path, with no clear idea of how they got there and no map for getting back to where they want to be. We want to help you get back on course.

A CHILD NO MORE

There comes a time when each of us must put away childish things and enter adulthood. Usually that happens in adolescence. Little Jimmy wants to be called James now, and little Mary's wearing makeup and a bra. Maybe they don't want to go to Chuck E. Cheese this time, but Alfredo's sounds nice. "Mommy" is no longer heard in your house, only "Mom" or "Mother."

Adolescence is that wonderfully mixed time when they have to pay adult price for a movie ticket, but they can't get in without Mom or Dad. They can kill and die for their country three years before they can have a glass of wine. We're neither advocating nor criticizing these activities; we're merely saying that teenagers are straining to leave childhood and become adults but are finding it difficult. Sometimes the only cure for the already/not-yet tension of adolescence is to just keep having birthdays.

It stands to reason that adolescents will want to move away from the structures and activities of childhood. This is healthy. They're not ten anymore. Children are supposed to grow up. You might need to change how you think about your young person and let the child go. Then learn to appreciate the budding adult in your home.

But a step away from childhood does not necessitate a step away from parents. In strong families, teens transform their relationships with their parents; they do not abandon them. Parents learn to lead not by their authority but by their influence, and teens learn to play the game of adulthood little by little. In the end, both parents and teens are completed adults. And hopefully they are friends.

ONE SIZE FITS ALL

This book is written for two types of readers. First, it is for parents who find themselves lost and in trouble, with teens in a state of relational tension (rebellion). These readers may pick up *On Becoming Teenwise* in desperation, fervently hoping it will be the navigational chart that can lead them to a better destination than the one they seem to be headed for.

If this is you, be assured that we offer in these pages an explanation of where relational tension with teens does and doesn't come from, what to do about it, and directions for how to get your family headed back toward earth.

This book is also written for families in which all is going well. These readers' children have entered or are on the brink of adolescence, and the journey seems to be moving along nicely, thank you very much. These readers want to know how to maintain this smooth sailing through what is reportedly a turbulent age. Perhaps they have raised their children with the whole On Becoming series, beginning with On Becoming Babywise, and simply want to keep a good thing going.

If this is you, you can rest assured that you'll find what you're looking for, too. Though adolescence be uncharted territory, we will be your guides, pointing out natural wonders and steering you past unmarked dangers. You, too, will benefit from understanding the source of relational tension with teens and how to generate a healthy family identity.

We have always maintained a positive outlook toward the teen years. Through our parenting seminars and Dr. Bucknam's medical practice, we have worked with thousands of families with teenagers, including our own. Gary Ezzo has an M.A. in Ministry, and Dr. Bucknam is a pediatrician with an eight thousand-patient list. With a little help here and a little tweaking there, tens of thousands of parents worldwide are enjoying glorious teen years with their children. Families have found our teachings substantial enough to enable them to realize a type of family harmony that is absolutely unheard of in a hostile society in which so many other families are falling apart.

The goal for all *Teenwise* readers is this: to find at the end of your childrearing years that your grown children have become your best friends. That's where we're headed.

THE VIEW FROM UP HERE

Let's look out the porthole and see where we are in relation to the earth and moon and how we're going to get to that ideal destination where you and your grown children will be fast friends.

In section 1 we'll look at the causes of relational tension with teens. We hear all the time that defiance in these years is just a given, that it's a natural—even healthy—part of growing up. We hear about hormones and peers and media and the effects of broken homes. We hear about smart sounding syndromes and disorders. We'll examine these components carefully, sorting the true from the false, beginning with an assessment test to help you know where you really are with your teen. Here's a peek: It is our belief that rebellion hassles and disruptive mood swings are *not* inescapable characteristics of the teen years.

In section 2 we'll cover how to parent teenagers in the trials of real life. This is where we talk about how to stop going the wrong direction and get turned around to the right heading. We'll show how to spot damage you may have contributed to yourself and what to do to fix it. The hard truth is that parents must bear some of the responsibility if conflict exists or if a teen is relationally disruptive. We'll talk about how to build a great relationship with your teen, and we'll give you tools for keeping it strong.

Section 3 leads you into those fantastic teen years. Did you think they were going to be terrible? Fear not! They can be great. We'll show you how in this section. This is the most exciting part of the book because here we get to talk about how to make your family the warm, uplifting place it can truly be. We'll talk about moral maturity, family identity, and how to get teens to invest in the family instead of looking elsewhere to belong. This is where it starts looking like friendship with your grown children might happen in your home after all. We'll also cover dating, courtship, and how to know if your teen is ready for marriage.

Section 4 is a special reference resource covering everything from sex and drugs to peer pressure, eating disorders, and spirituality. It is all-new material compiled just for *On Becoming Teenwise*. We think you'll find this section alone is worth the price of the book.

COUNTDOWN

The teen years don't have to be a terrible time of strife and tension. Other parents—including the Ezzos and now the Bucknams—have made it and are making it through their children's teen years without these symptoms. Young people in other eras and cultures have moved from childhood to adulthood without these troubles. And your family can, too.

Even if you feel like you're 380,000 miles from earth.

SECTION ONE

A QUESTION OF DEFIENCE

Chapter One

Where Are We?

Two tourists were driving through Louisiana. As they approached Natchitoches, they started arguing about the pronunciation of the name of the town. They argued back and forth until they stopped for lunch. As they stood at the counter, one tourist asked the employee, "Before we order, could you please settle an argument for us? Would you please pronounce where we are...very slowly?"

The girl leaned over the counter and said, "Burrrrrrrr-gerrrrrrr Kiiiiiing."

YOU ARE HERE

When it comes to raising teenagers, sometimes we just don't know where we are. We may have loud and clear evidence indicating we're not where we want to be, but O what we wouldn't give for a GPS downlink and a map.

All parent/teen relationships can be placed somewhere on a scale of good and bad, rapport or conflict. If you're having very few problems with your teenager, or if the problems you're having are no worse than getting her to make her bed in the morning, you're very close to the rapport side of the scale. If your son has a drug problem and the police are asking where your daughter is, you're probably closer to the conflict side.

Rapport ————————————————————— Conflict

Keep this scale in mind when you're having difficulties with your teen. It may seem like an impossible problem to you that your son will never put gas in the car. But when you realize that that's a minor problem compared to the parent whose teen has had an abortion, it can help you keep your perspective.

TESTING, TESTING, ONE, TWO, THREE

Take the following assessment test to see where you are in your parent/teen relationship. This will help you place your family on the rapport/conflict scale. If you answer according to what is actually true most of the time in your home (as opposed to what you wish were true or what was true one Saturday a year ago), you will discover where you really are with your teenager.

Mulling over the many questionnaires completed by parents across the country, we discovered that parents tend to grade themselves unfairly. Parents with "good" kids were often harder on themselves, earning worse scores than what their real situations merited. Conversely, struggling parents tended to underrate the seriousness of their problems or contradict themselves. Some answered, "Yes, my son is on drugs," but also answered, "Yes, my son has strong moral convictions." It hurts to give answers that drive home the reality of a struggling relationship. But there is also great hope in beginning the process. In order to gain optimum help, please aim for brutal honesty.

Do this test for each teenager in your home. For personal enlightenment, consider taking the test on behalf of your own parents. How do you think they would've answered these questions about you way back when?

YOU MAY OPEN YOUR TEST PACKET

Write your responses in the spaces adjacent to each question in this section, basing your answers on the following 1–5 scale:

1 = This rarely, if ever, is true of our teen or our relationship.

2 = This is not usually true of our teen or our relationship.

3 = Sometimes this is true of our teen or our relationship, but just as often is not.

4 = This usually represents our teen or our relationship.

5 = This perfectly represents our teen or our relationship.

1.___ Our teen is interested in what is going on in our lives.

2.___ For his or her age, we feel confident in our teen's ability to make wise decisions for him- or herself.

3.___ Our teen considers us to be part of his or her inner circle of best friends.

4.___ Our teen doesn't often say things like, "I can't wait until I'm old enough to move out of this house."

5.___ Our teen picks up after him- or herself.

6.___ If our teen had a choice, he or she would choose us to be his or her parents.

7.___ Our teen's friends consider our family fun to be with.

8.___ If we were going away for the weekend, I know we could trust our teen to stay home alone.

9.___ Our teen does not think we are overly critical of him or her.

10.___ In some families, if it weren't for sports or the weather, parents probably wouldn't have anything to talk about with their teen. We're so thankful that's not the case in our family.

11.___ Our teen considers us to be fair and flexible.

12.___ Our teen accepts criticism, evaluates it, and is willing to talk about it.

13.___ Our teen can accept no for an answer without blowing up.

14.___ We are seeing signs of advanced moral maturity in our teen.

15.___ Our teen considers us to be a good source of counsel.

16.___ Our parent/teen communication is characterized by very few limitations. We can talk about anything.

17.___ When we ask our teen to do something, we never worry that he or she will run away.

18.___ Our teen would never physically threaten us.

19.___ Our adult friends enjoy our teen.

20.___ Our teen doesn't have the attitude that everyone else can pick up after him or her.

21.___ By their behavior, some teens put stress on their whole family. Our teen's behavior doesn't escalate stress in our home—quite the opposite, actually.

22.___ Our teen feels we appreciate him or her.

23.___ We've really learned to lead less by our authority ("Because

I said so!") and more by the attractiveness of our relationship with our teen.

24.___ Our teen is not easily influenced by his or her peers or by trendy styles or behaviors.

25.___ If we were running late and left the dinner dishes on the table, our teen would probably clean the table, wash the dishes, and put them away.

26.___ Our teen is often sought out as a baby-sitter.

27.___ We're confident that our teen is not sexually active.

28.___ Our teen knows that if we wrong him or her in any way, he or she can count on an apology from us.

29.___ Our teen prefers spending more time with our family than with his or her friends.

30.___ Our teen respects the limits we set.

31.___ When we have a disagreement with our teen, we make up quickly without harboring a grudge.

32.___ Our teen will never agree with what we say one minute, then go do what he or she wants the next.

33.___ Our teen would be one of the sources of counsel that we would seek out in a time of crisis.

34.___ Our teen's taste in clothing and hairstyle is compatible with (not necessarily identical to) ours.

35.___ We have more influence over our teen than his or her peers do.

36.___ We're confident that our teen is not experimenting or has not experimented with drugs.

37.___ When our teen comes home late, we know he or she will have a legitimate reason.

38.___ Our teen looks forward to special family times when it is just us together.

39.___ When we ask our teen to do something, we never end up in a power struggle.

40.___ If we get into an argument, our teen doesn't go silent for hours or days.

Name of Teen _____Score _____

Name of Teen _____Score _____

Name of Teen _____Score _____

SCORING INTERPRETATION

40–60   Parent/teen relationship is nonexistent.

61–80   Barely tolerable parent/teen relationship.

81–115   Weak parent/teen relationship, characterized by conflict.

116–140   Okay-to-weak parent/teen relationship. There are some behavioral concerns that if not corrected, could lead to struggles and conflict.

141–170   Healthy parent/teen relationship with minor problems.

171–200   Very healthy parent/teen relationship.

EVALUATION

Well, how did you do? By identifying the strengths and weaknesses of your relationship with your teen, you have gained a great advantage in parenting. When you understand the information we'll give in the next chapters, you can begin working objectively toward reinforcing the positive aspects of your teen's character while shoring up the weak ones.

But even with this advantage, please understand that neither your teen nor you will ever be perfect. The teen years will not be bump free even if you maxed out on this test. Regardless of how many books you read, seminars you attend, or tests you take, you're not going to do it right all the time. No one can. And that's okay as long as you're doing it right more and more of the time.

SUMMARY

This chapter is designed to give you a reference point, not to condemn you. Many public schools give a test at the beginning of the year, then give the same test at the end. The idea is to show how much the children have improved. Let this chapter serve as the tool to measure the improvement you will see in your family after you've learned and implemented the principles in this book.

BRINGING IT HOME

Take some time now to discuss this chapter with your spouse. Talk about how you scored on the test and what you think you could do better, even now. Then ask each other this question: Where do we want to be in our parent/teen relationship in five years?

Begin to form a shared vision for what you want your family relationships to look like in the future and steps you might take to get there. The remainder of this book will help flesh out your vision. It's amazing how helpful it is to have a plan.

Chapter Two

What Society Says About the Problem

*W*hen it comes to explaining things, people can get very creative. Just take these notes sent to excuse students from school:

- Please excuse Johnnie for being. It was his father's fault.
- George was absent yesterday because he had a stomach.
- Please excuse Sara for being absent. She was sick and I had her shot.
- Ralph was absent yesterday because he had a sore trout.

There are just as many theories out there to explain why teenagers go astray. A few are as imaginative as the excuses above. Some people say rebellion is caused by hormones; some say it's caused by the media; some say it's just a natural part of growing up. We hear it must be genetics or a lack of self-esteem or the result of some exotic syndrome. It's parents' too-strict limitations that have caused the behavior—or the lack of any restraint whatsoever. It's because he was underattached, overattached, or wasn't breast-fed long enough. It's the result of improper self-discovery or a fear of abandonment caused by that time you left him with the sitter when he was two.

Some of these explanations seem to be attempts by parents to evade responsibility for their teen's misbehavior. Others seem to say that the parents are completely to blame, and the poor child is just misunderstood. How can we separate the silver from the dross?

We'll take a look at these theories in a moment. First, let's examine what teen rebellion (we prefer the term *relational tension*) looks like. Once you learn to recognize it, you're well on the way to dealing with it.

A REBEL BY ANY OTHER NAME

When we talk about relational tension in teenagers, we mean the teen displays a willful desire to overthrow family leadership and a willingness to walk away from relational accountability.

Relational tension, though it may have many external influences, ultimately arises from human nature. All of us want to get our way. When some power or authority comes in and thwarts us from having our way, we get mad. We fight to overcome that force so that we can get what we want.

Each of us handles this conflict differently. Some struggle with the force that opposes them, but when it cannot be overcome, they comply. Others, when they come to the realization that they can't defeat the authority, flee. Those who flee are usually running from one of three things: a social obligation, a responsibility, or a relationship. Teenagers tend to flee from relationships, which comes out in the form of rebellion.

Even if your teen is a regular in the principal's office or is having run-ins with the police, we believe the ultimate source of the relational tension is a deficiency in the parent/teen relationship. If that's not healthy, teens will rebel against it, and a host of other problems will logically follow.

Nevertheless, parents tend to look for other explanations for their teen's behavior, things that will show that it wasn't anything they've done or failed to do. Let's look at some of the candidates.

THE USUAL SUSPECTS

When a crime is committed by an unknown assailant in a high-crime district, the police pull in the usual suspects for questioning and for a witness lineup. Many times the real culprit isn't among that group, after all, but it's always a good place to start.

So now, when we're trying to deduce who or what is responsible for teenage rebellion, we're going to haul in the usual suspects—the explanations usually offered—for examination. We don't believe the offender is here, but since these are such popular answers in our society, we thought this would be a good place to start.

In chapter 3 we will talk about what things we think work together to cause teen rebellion. If you can't stand the suspense and just have to find out now, we hereby give you permission to jump ahead. Just promise to come back so we can get on with the investigation.

THEORY ONE: HORMONES

Your fourteen-year-old son is starting to pay more attention to his grooming because of a dawning attraction to the opposite sex. His preferences in music and hairstyle are beginning to reflect what his peers like more than what you like. You're beginning to have conflict over his after-school whereabouts. You want him home working on his school projects; he wants to be at the mall. His attitude and tone toward you have changed for the worse. The battles have begun, and back and forth you go.

Your fifteen-year-old daughter feels bloated during her period. She's become dissatisfied with her appearance and is pushing herself into a semistarvation pattern of eating. Alarmed at her weight loss, you try to force her to eat. This just pushes her to go throw up when she thinks you don't know. Tension builds and daily arguments ensue.

Is testosterone to blame for your son's attitude problems? Are hormones making your daughter a little crazy? Tantrums, defiance, eating disorders—indeed, all the problems commonly encountered in adolescence—are often explained away as the result of hormonal changes in a young person's body. It's the terrible twos back with a wallop. Their poor behavior is excused as completely natural, just a phase all teens have to go through. But is this really what is at the root of the trouble? American society would say yes. We say, probably not.

To be sure, hormones are operating in overdrive during the teen years. They do affect behavior and attitudes to some degree. But the crucial question is this: Do hormonal changes cause your children to make bad choices?

We should point out that there are legitimate medical problems associated with hormonal imbalances. An excess or deficiency of one or more of the hormones produced by the glands of the endocrine system can affect personality. A hyperthyroid condition, for example, can make a child nervous, excited, jumpy, restless, and overactive. A hypothyroid condition, on the other hand, causes children to be lethargic, unresponsive, dissatisfied, even depressed.

Nor are teens the only ones affected by hormones. Just consider a woman in menopause. She will experience hot flashes, sweating, dryness, burning, and itching—all legitimate results of hormonal change. But if this fortysomething mother of three tossed her apron, hopped on a Harley, and headed for Alaska, could she blame it on hormones? No. She would be making a choice. Her actions would have happened during the midst of hormonal flux, but they would hardly have been caused by it.

Nevertheless, some parents make the same mistake, blaming their teen's misbehavior on hormonal changes that happened at the same time as their misbehavior but which were not the cause of it.

Supporters of the hormone-induced rebellion theory suggest that hormonal changes substantially increase a teen's tendency to rebel and reject the values of his or her family. They almost seem to believe that what the endocrine system produces is not estrogen or testosterone but pure, liquid defiance—rebellion juice.

If it were true that the endocrine system's release of hormones into the body automatically triggered rebellion, then this kind of rebellion would begin at age seven since that's when hormonal changes begin. The new growth period marks the end of a hormonal suppression set in place soon after birth and the beginning of many years of glandular arousal. At age seven, the gonadotrophin hormone levels begin to rise in both boys and girls. By age twelve this process has been in full swing for several years.

Therefore, if a child hits twelve or thirteen and suddenly starts defying authority, there is no reason to blame hormones.

(By the way, we won't be discussing "the talk," when you tell your child about his or her burgeoning sexuality, in this book. We covered that at length in *On Becoming Preteen Wise*. But here are three guidelines: It's best to do it along gender lines (fathers with sons, mothers with daughters); you don't have to do it all at once, but it can and should be an open, ongoing dialogue; and it is sometimes helpful to use a book on the subject as an aid—just be sure to go through that book with your child instead of leaving it for him or her to find and blunder through alone. Okay, back to hormones.)

Glandular surges do not cause children to lie, steal, cheat, act disrespectfully, defy authority, or relationally wander away from their parents. Hormones may affect the human body, but not the human heart.

If hormones caused rebellion:

- the problem would be universal. The genetic time clock would kick in at essentially the same time for children in all societies and cultures, bringing about rebellion in adolescents across the globe. Just the thought of it would keep us awake nights. Thankfully, it doesn't happen this way.
- how do we explain the healthy families whose teens don't rebel? These kids go through the same hormonal changes but do not seek to overthrow their parents' leadership.
- why isn't medication its cure?

WHAT SOCIETY SAYS ABOUT TEENAGE REBELLION

Hormones are unquestionably at work during the teen years. They add to the energy and awkwardness and even stress of adolescents. But they should not be allowed to excuse bad behavior any more than having a bad day at work excuses child abuse. Teenagers retain their ability—and their responsibility—to make good choices and keep their attitudes in check.

THEORY TWO: SEEKING INDEPENDENCE

You and your thirteen-year-old daughter seem to clash all the time these days. You've heard that daughters just have to disagree with mothers as part of growing up, and you remember something from psychology class that says sons have to "murder" the father figure to become men themselves. So you're pretty sure that the constant disagreements with your own teen are just a case of her seeking to become her own person, separate from her parents.

The theory goes like this: Adolescence is the period when children attempt to separate themselves from the parental bonds of love and dependence and move toward an adult identity. It is another attempt to explain why a teenager would close his or her heart toward Mom and Dad during the teen years. These kids aren't rebelling, the theory goes, they're simply striving for independence. They are "planting their flag," declaring themselves independent and sovereign. This tearing away is said to be necessary in order for the child to become an adult.

In one sense, this is certainly true: A teenager is experiencing a rebirth. He is coming out of the cocoon of childhood and beginning to explore his world and his self. He's considering for himself who he wants to be rather than simply being a child. He's able to make informed decisions, decisions that may differ from what his parents would choose. He's seeking independence from the things of childhood. There is an invigorating sense of self-determination during the teen years in which the young person feels he is master of his own destiny.

(There is another scenario in which teens might be rightly desiring independence from parents: when there are unhealthy relationships at home. More on this in chapter 3.)

The independence notion is rooted in the Freudian theory of the personality. According to Freud, a child's quest to be detached from parental control is the root cause of teenage rebellion. And since Freud's legacy is alive and well today, many parents now believe that rebellion isn't a question of *if* but of *when*.

The idea that rebellion is necessary in order for a child to become an adult offers a false sense of comfort to bewildered parents, freeing them from accountability for their teen's behavior. However, it also can discourage parents, causing many to give up before they start. If parents believe that no matter what they do in the early years, conflict is unavoidable, it adds up to a lose-lose situation for the family.

Adolescence *is* a time of self-discovery. But discovery doesn't have to mean defiance. A young person discovering she likes soccer, even though her parents don't, isn't defying her parents by kicking a ball. Now, we suppose someone might use soccer as a way to hurt her parents, but we shouldn't assume that every player on the field is out there to spite Mom and Dad.

Teens don't have to become something their parents dislike in order to be their own individuals. If that were so, a teen wouldn't be unique; he would just be a mirror image of his parents. If Mom and Dad were conservative, Junior would *have* to be liberal, or he would just be his parents' clone. We don't think it has to be this way. Teens do need to find out who they want to be, but they should be free to select qualities and values held by their parents as well as those not held by them.

In our opinion, reaching adulthood does not require relational tension. Defiance of authority is not a growing pain but a behavioral choice. Rebelling against parents doesn't make you an adult any more than rebelling against a government makes you president.

THEORY THREE: POOR SELF-ESTEEM

A third theory often given for why teenagers rebel involves the role of self-esteem. Many believe that a lack of positive self-esteem is the root cause of teens doing drugs, experiencing academic failure, participating in gang violence, becoming sexually active, and rebelling against their parents.

In America, self-esteem enhancement is everywhere. We read about it, hear it over the radio, watch it on sitcoms, learn it in the classroom, and move to its music. Contemporary sociologists, psychologists, and educators alike say that a child's happiness, success, physical coordination, and, yes, even IQ hinge upon a healthy self-esteem.

Now, to be sure, self-esteem plays a role. A teen who feels worthless is likely to act out in any number of disruptive ways. (On the other hand, a teen who feels superior to everyone else is just as unpleasant to be around.) But wait: Does a poor self-esteem excuse defiant, disrespectful, or illegal actions? Should someone be acquitted of a crime because he was feeling bad about himself when he committed it? Is feeling good the prerequisite for doing good?

Parents working under the theory that self-esteem is the Holy Grail of child-rearing become slaves to whatever it takes to make the child feel good about himself. They work tirelessly to ensure that children have the right activities, the right clothes, the right car, the biggest party, a "cool" dad who lets anything go, and the "supermom" who strives to create utopia for the kids. Parents feel they must maximize the child's pleasure and minimize his pain, or he'll end up being a menace to society.

To be fair, most parents who ascribe to this theory love their children greatly and sincerely think this is the way to help them succeed in life. Parents often strive selflessly to make sure their children have what they need for healthy self-esteem. But gallant as this effort may be, we still have to ask if it was necessary in the first place. It may seem heroic to dive into a pool after a drowning child, but any lifeguard will tell you that using a long pole would have been smarter.

Does good self-esteem produce healthy development in children, or does healthy development produce within children a satisfying sense of self? If it's the former, then mainstream America is right in its efforts to enhance warm fuzzies. But if the latter is true, if indeed the effort to raise self-esteem is actually contributing to America's teen problem, then we need to change course in a hurry.

We believe it's backwards to say that feeling good is the precursor to doing good. If the child's got to feel good before he'll act correctly, all misbehavior is really the parent's fault. If he throws his cereal bowl on the carpet, it's because Mommy hasn't made him feel happy. If she looks right at you while doing something you told her not to, it's your fault somehow. No wonder parents are enslaved to keeping their children appeased: They perceive misbehavior as parental failure.

We take an approach that would liberate these parents. We believe that *doing good leads to feeling good*. Right behavior leads to right feelings, and the accumulation of right feelings leads to a healthy view of self.

When you do the right thing, you feel approved, appreciated, virtuous—even when no one is looking. That's because your conscience, the silent witness of your soul, speaks to you either by affirming or accusing you regarding your actions. This is the basis for the statement, "Do something good; feel something real."

When you do a good deed or perform your civic duty or return to pay for that item you accidentally walked out of the store with, don't you feel good about yourself? Doing right leads to feeling right.

Though it might be surprising to hear, we've found that parents who place a greater emphasis on how a child feels than on how he acts experience a higher rate of teenage rebellion. It makes sense, though, doesn't it? If the highest good is a child who feels happy and pleased with himself, then anything that detracts from that feeling would be considered bad.

So, when Mom asks thirteen-year-old Chris to take out the trash, Chris lets her know that such a chore would make him feel neither happy nor pleased with himself. Mom feels guilty pressing anything on him that will wound his fragile self-esteem, so she relents. Or else she forces him to do it, which elicits great defiance from Chris. And why not, since he's come to believe that life is all about what makes him happy and that his parents' job is to see that he's kept that way?

What an irony! The very parents who work so hard to enhance their children's self-image actually end up creating the menaces to society they sought to eliminate. The more they feed the greed, the more the greed grows until they find they've raised greedy, selfish, ungrateful children who think the world ought to bend over backward to make them feel good.

In these families parent/teen conflict appears to rise proportionately to the emphasis given to early self-esteem training. More focus on good feelings equals more relational tension in the teen years.

Put your emphasis on leading your teen to do good because doing good leads to feeling good.

THEORY FOUR: SYNDROMES AND DISORDERS

We hear about so many psychological syndromes and disorders: attachment syndrome, child depression, children's bipolar syndrome, ADD, ADHD, and oppositional behavior disorder. Today, when the psychologist is high priest, parents often feel that whatever strange behavior their teen exhibits must be the result of some neurosis or chemical imbalance.

There are children and teenagers who truly do struggle with legitimate mental and emotional disorders. You may, in fact, wish to have your teen evaluated. You can also find out about all of these maladies on the Internet and in your public library. But beware of looking for labels to justify misbehavior. We feel it is too much to lump every occurrence of antisocial behavior into the category of psychological disorders.

It's tempting to look to some kind of syndrome as the explanation for why our teenagers behave badly. It reassures us that we couldn't have done anything to prevent it. But defiance is fundamentally a heart issue. It certainly can be influenced by the strengths and weaknesses of personality and temperament and maybe even neurological deficiencies. But the bottom line is that it's a moral choice. If we choose to forget that, then even the most bizarre explanations become acceptable.

There is one common thread among most of these disorders: a lack of healthy sleep patterns. Before you take your child to a psychologist or therapist, and definitely before someone starts to prescribe a little white pill, maybe what you want to do is take him to someone who's involved in sleep research. Your family's physician should be able to make a recommendation.

A friend of ours, a top researcher in sleep disorders, is finding a significant increase in the percentage of teens who cannot sleep through the night. Because he's familiar with our teachings in our On Becoming series of child-rearing books, he's made a point of checking *Childwise* kids against kids who have not been raised that way. He has found that *Childwise* kids tend to have healthy sleep patterns and, perhaps consequently, tend not to have ADD or other behavioral disorders.

Proper nutrition is another key to good emotional health. If your teen is subsisting on Twinkies and Taco Bell, that might be a clue for you. So before you take your teenager to a psychologist, make sure he is keeping good dietary habits and sleeping at least seven hours every night.

If you give good diet and healthy sleep a chance to work (a month or more) and you've seen no improvement, and you're sure your teen is not just lacking self-control or a sense of responsibility, then perhaps it is time to turn to someone who can give you an evaluation.

That doesn't necessarily mean going to a professional. Parents who have successfully guided their teens through situations like this are your best therapists. Before you spend any money, find someone in your church, synagogue, or community who has already been where you are. Find out how they handled it and what happened as a result. You especially want to find families who have gone through it and have found tremendous success on the other end. These folks have experience, but they don't have a billing system.

If you do take your teen to a professional counselor, our recommendation is that you not take the first opinion that comes down the road. Be sure to get at least two opinions. Be very, very hesitant to put your teen on medication. Chemically subduing your teen is never preferable to solving the problem that's behind the behavior.

SUMMARY

Teenagers do not usually rebel against authority; they rebel against relationships. They're not rebelling because it's their nature, because they're driven by hormones, or because they've got a disorder. They're rebelling because there is within every human a natural selfishness that makes us want to defy anyone or anything that's going to take away our self-governance.

Teenage rebellion is an unfortunate fact of life in America. But it doesn't have to happen in your home. Just because something is common doesn't mean it's inevitable. Statistically, divorce is common, too. However, most couples don't marry fully intending to divorce later. In the same way, you don't have to expect that growth from childhood to adulthood must result in a fractured relationship with your teen.

In our next chapter, we'll talk about what we think is the real source of teenage rebellion.

BRINGING IT HOME

1. When is relational tension created?
2. Do hormones cause teens to make bad choices?
3. In healthy families, what are teens seeking independence from?
4. In families where parent/teen tension exists, what are teens seeking independence from?
5. Is feeling good the precursor to doing good? If not, what is the correct sequence?

Chapter Three

The Real Causes of Teenage Rebellion

C arolyn was in complete rebellion. She and her boyfriend were sexually active. She admitted to experimenting with drugs and had even taken money from her parents to finance her growing habit. She was fiercely defiant and expressed that in her dress, speech, actions, and whereabouts.

Her parents were desperate. They read every book about teen psychology they could get their hands on. They bought her extravagant gifts and bankrolled international vacations. They took her to seminars and counseling. Nothing seemed to work. In the end they shipped Carolyn off to an aunt in Los Angeles, if for no other reason than to get her away from her boyfriend and drug suppliers.

Just a rebellious daughter, right? An adolescent simply going through a phase. Her hormones were going wild, and she was expressing her newfound independence. Maybe she had ADHD or needed to have more space to find her own way.

That's what people were telling Carolyn's parents. They were probably telling Carolyn the same thing. Just ride it out—or write her off. But when friends asked the Ezzos to personally intervene, Gary and Anne Marie discovered a very different reality. (If you can't wait, jump to the end of the chapter, then come back.)

RECIPE FOR REBELLION

In chapter 2 we talked about the reasons society gives to explain relational tension with teens. Each theory contained some truth and did explain some cases of defiance but was found to be deficient for explaining the epidemic of rebellion we see in homes across this country. Even taken together, they can explain perhaps only 15 percent of the relational tension in teens in America. What causes the rest? That's what this chapter is all about.

REBOOT

Let's say you're working at your personal computer at the office. It's using Microsoft Windows to run your word processing software, spreadsheets, databases, and other applications. After you've been working for a while, you begin to get strange messages from your computer. Programs start behaving poorly and doing bizarre things. Error messages you've never seen and couldn't decipher if your life depended on it begin cascading across your monitor. Finally, the whole thing locks up.

You click around for a bit but can't make any progress. Since you know a thing or two about Windows, you press Ctrl-Alt-Del. But nothing happens. Try as you might, you can't recover. It's a total system crash. In the end, your only recourse is to turn the computer off and begin again.

Chances are, things were going wrong long before you became

aware of it. Windows is fairly tolerant of errors and internal conflicts. Alone, none of the little problems was enough to bring the system to a screeching halt. Even with two or four or eight minor problems going on behind the scenes, the computer was still able to perform well enough for you to keep working.

But eventually the errors accumulated to the point where Windows' tolerance was exceeded, and the whole thing crashed. That lockup was probably your first clue that anything was wrong at all.

The beauty of personal computers is that no matter how bad the crash was before, a simple reset is usually enough to wipe everything clean and let you go back to stable, productive computing.

Families of teens can be the same way. Little problems can go unnoticed. Minor disturbances can hide below the surface. None by itself is enough to cause a major crisis. But when enough factors and glitches accumulate, one final problem can trigger a massive blowup. In some families, the explosion is the first hint anyone has that something is seriously wrong.

Happily, families can be reset, too. No matter how tangled the mess or scorched the feelings, families with teenagers can begin anew.

In this chapter we'll discuss factors that contribute to teenage rebellion. Together, two or more of these can accumulate into trouble. Section 2 will explore how to reset the machine. And sections 3 and 4 will set you on your way to happy family networking.

CONTRIBUTING FACTOR ONE: THE ABSENCE OF MORAL COMMUNITY

Today we live in a society that is hostile toward the family. Parents who want to raise moral children are virtually at war with the community in which they live.

This was not always the case. Fifty years ago a shared Judeo-Christian ethic produced social unity. At that time even bad parents could raise good children because society acted as a safety net to catch kids when moms and dads failed. Neighbors, teachers, little league coaches, and the community at large provided the moral direction the child wasn't getting at home. This is what a common moral community looks like.

Today common moral communities are virtually nonexistent. That is why good parents can still turn out a wayward child. Let that be an encouragement to you: Sometimes the best parents in the world can still end up with defiant teens. Without a moral community reinforcing the values you're teaching at home, you must fight alone against television, pornography, drugs, premarital sex, vulgar public advertising, degrading schools, and negative peer pressure.

There is still a community out there, and it still exerts pressure on teens, but the direction it urges them has shifted 180 degrees. Now parents are expected and even encouraged to support their teen's rebellion. It's almost as if families everywhere are trying to excuse the rebellion in their own homes by being sure it's in yours, too. It's presented as a rite of passage for parents, just as some people look forward to their "first divorce."

With no moral community to support it, a family trying to raise a teen not to rebel may feel a bit like an ice cube trying to stay frozen in the middle of the Mojave Desert. Hostile environments take their toll.

Connecting with a Moral Community

Since members of your community are going to teach your children, directly or indirectly, it is vital that you surround yourself with people who share your morals and values. In a moral community you will find people who are striving to live out respect and honor and instill moral awareness and consideration for others in their children. These are the people who can provide a support group for you, Mom and Dad.

Your teenager will find his or her friends in your community. You want those to be moral kids—kids whose parents are working to instill values in their hearts just as you are with your teen. A like-minded moral community is vital.

The greater the disparity between the values of your family and your community, the greater the source of conflict within the home. The opposite is also true: Shared values between community and home result in positive peer pressure on your young person.

Take a moment to think about the moral environment in which you and your teen live. Is there a discrepancy between the moral level you hope to instill in your teens and the moral level of those in your circle of relations? If not, could you make a change that would help?

We're not suggesting you move into a monastery, but maybe something less drastic would still be beneficial. Could you move to a smaller town or better part of town? Could you put your teen in a private school? Could you join a church that has a strong youth program? Could you take a job that would allow you more time alone with your teenager? You never know how effective such a change might be in helping you get back on track with your teen.

How and Where to Find a Moral Community

There are moral communities out there. If you know **where** to look, they're easy to find. Churches and synagogues are obvious starting points. The Judeo-Christian tradition is based on a moral code. Find one close to your teen's school, and he's sure to find friends from class there.

Look around the next time you go to your teen's football game or dance recital. Do you see kids who behave like you'd like your teen to behave? Find out where they are and where they go. Strike up conversations with their parents. When you find kids whose attitudes are appealing to you, they are likely to be part of a like-minded community—a community you and your teenager could join.

By urging you to surround your family with people who share your values, we are not suggesting that you should isolate your children from the rest of society. That, in our opinion, is going too far. However, we do want to insulate our children from corruptive influences.

The Ezzos recently moved their offices to a new facility. For a couple of weeks they worked in offices with no office walls. The only things that separated the offices from one another were air and metal studs placed every twenty-four inches. There was no escape from voices, printers, keyboards, and the occasional smell of someone's chili burger. Eventually, one side of the wall went up. While that kept the chili burger aroma out, the noise level continued to be bothersome. It wasn't until the insulation and wallboard went up between the offices that individuals were protected from unwanted elements.

By the same token, a moral community insulates your teens against the elements of the world. Through association with like-minded peers, your teenagers will see family standards reinforced by others who share the same values. The strength they draw from moral peers is the very thing that makes it possible for you as parents to let them participate in extracurricular activities.

Plug into a moral community this week.

CONTRIBUTING FACTOR TWO: MEDIA—MUSIC, TV, INTERNET, MOVIES

"My son's a media junkie," one mother said. "As soon as he gets up, he's got VH-1 turned on in his room. After breakfast he's on the computer. He says he's just checking his e-mail, but his little sister tells me that's not all he's doing. I can still hear the rap music pounding through the ground after his car has pulled out of the driveway. When he comes home from school, it's the same in reverse, with video games, band magazines, and the occasional almost X-rated movie thrown in, too.

"If I ever dare ask him to do a chore or spend time with the family, you would think that I'd asked him to cut off his hand. I don't mind music and movies and all, but I wish they didn't seem to be standing between him and me."

Today we live in the latter stages of the information revolution. Our lives are saturated with print and electronic media. If we let it, it will occupy every waking moment of our lives.

Though media choices come up in many parent/teen conflicts, we do not believe radio, movies, TV, magazines, the Internet, and the rest *cause* rebellion in teens. The offensive media choices teens make are usually symptoms of something deeper. However, we do believe the media of our culture feed rebellion and encourage its growth. Media's message is often subtly degrading. It can act to distance teens from their family's common moral stance, further deconstructing already unstable relationships.

Mass media, particularly that connected with the music scene, can provide an identity for a young person who hasn't been given one in his family. Without a family identity at home and a moral community reinforcing it, teens can feel they don't know who they are. Popular media provide an answer. Chances are, though, you won't be pleased with the identity your teenager adopts from MTV.

When parents begin to investigate media's role in relational tension between them and their teens, we always urge them to consider the context they have provided in their homes. Are parents bothered that their teens are watching near-porn on cable, but they think it's fine to let them watch R-rated movies that depict sexual activity? Are parents upset that their teens are investigating the occult, but they don't bat an eyelid when they play with preoccult toys or games like *Magic: The Gathering, Pokémon,* and *Dungeons & Dragons?* Parents who establish a certain tolerance for immorality in the home shouldn't be surprised when their teens just want to take the next logical step. That statement is not meant to accuse but to point out that a little leaven leavens the whole lump.

Another thing to guard against is trying to make common tastes, rather than common values, the foundation for family identity. Whenever parents try to make their teens conform to a fixed set of preferences, they are almost guaranteed relational tension in the home. Is it really so bad that you like opera and your daughter likes ska? It would be ridiculous for parents to demand that their children all prefer the color green over any other color. In the same way, to demand that all favor the same tastes in music, movies, and dress would be to beg for conflict.

Virtues and morals, not enforced media preferences, ought to form the basis for a family's common ground. The greater the shared common values among family members, the less likely teenagers' preferences will scare you. Unite yourselves on the basis of values or else you will forever battle preferences and tastes in friends, music, clothing, and the rest.

Via Media: Countering Media's Effects

The first thing to do when you want to minimize media's negative effects is to be sure you've got the basics covered in your home. In section 2, we'll talk about having couch time with your spouse, creating heart-to-hearts with your teen, really talking and listening, building family identity, and seeking and granting forgiveness. If your teen has chosen media you disapprove of, putting these basics in place will very often cause the problem to fix itself.

Second, endeavor to be consistent with your messages. It's difficult to justify displeasure over the morality represented in your teen's media choices when your own choices are little different. Teens will appreciate it when you eliminate any actions that may seem hypocritical.

Third, be sure to offer alternatives. It probably won't work to just squelch the media choices your teen is making. Try something like this: "Son, instead of TV tonight, I've rented one of my favorite old movies for us to watch together." "Instead of your usual online chat, tonight I'd like us to all go to the mall for some window shopping and ice cream." It's natural to want to control something that seems out of control, but doing so without a release valve only creates frustration for everybody. (We'll cover the idea of substitution over suppression more fully in chapter 6.)

Finally, learn to accept some of your teen's media choices. If there's no moral reason why she shouldn't be watching it, reading it, or listening to it, and if it's not interfering with family priorities, maybe you can learn to live with it. You might even find you like it.

Media can contribute to relational tension in a family that is teetering on the edge. It can add fuel to the fire where rebellion is already burning brightly. But if kept within proper limits, it will not cause teen rebellion.

CONTRIBUTING FACTOR THREE: DIVORCE

The breakdown of family harmony during the teen years can be attributed to many factors. Mode and style of parenting, a weak marriage, drugs or alcohol abuse, parental manipulation, an overbearing mother, and an absentee father will all emotionally impact future family relationships. But the most painful relationship setback for children is divorce. The parents' subsequent remarriages only deepen the wound.

Many people say and apparently believe that divorce and remarriage do not have a negative impact on children. Children are emotionally resilient, they say. They'll "bounce back" from the trauma of separated parents.

They're not. They can't. Have you ever met anyone from a broken home who didn't have problems with relationships? Children of divorce will (usually) survive and maybe even come to thrive but not without deep wounds. Children pay a huge price for their parents' divorce.[1]

The rate of divorce is so high in the United States that now the family headed by original marriage partners is no longer the statistical norm. Some estimates put this group at slightly more than 40 percent of our family population.[2] This means the majority of families with teens are facing the added burden of absent parents and/or family blending.

In mentioning the impact divorce has on teen rebellion, we have no intention of condemning anyone's present circumstances. These remarks are intended to help single parents and blended-family parents understand the source of possible tension. And, perhaps, to encourage struggling couples to commit to working things out for the sake of their children if not for themselves.

From a teen's point of view, divorce violates the unspoken relationship covenant inherent in the family. With divorce comes a sense of betrayal. Despite what some writers have said, that sense of betrayal is worsened when parents remarry. Remarriage dashes a child's hope of seeing the family reunited and leaves him feeling emotionally abandoned. Most teens don't want to see another man become Dad or another woman become Mom so long as the biological parent waits in the wings.

The way a child responds to the pain of divorce depends on his or her age. Younger children tend to respond by withdrawing from life, while older children may respond with anger, disappointment, and finally, rejection of relationships. If a child has had a strong attachment to the biological parents, the possibility of teenage stress increases with divorce and remarriage. And a common way for teens to express stress is rebellion. Further, if the relationship with the stepparent is poor, there is the possibility for tragedy.

Divorce is terribly disruptive even to grown children. In most cases, the yawning chasm a child feels beneath him will cause him to act out in unpredictable ways. One of those ways may be rebellion, if only as an effort to call for your attention. Redouble your efforts to make your teen feel secure.

CONTRIBUTING FACTOR FOUR: CONFLICTING TEMPERAMENTS

"I don't understand it," a man confided over dinner. "Dad raised all five of us boys the same. So why did Jake turn out like he did? The four of us older brothers loved athletics, but Jake never did. We were all the starting quarterbacks in high school, but Jake got cut from the JV team. Dad's in ministry, and all four of us followed him, but Jake couldn't even sit still in church when Dad was preaching.

"Jake was rebellious from the beginning. He hated football, even though Dad made him play. It seemed like he detested everything Dad liked. When he was old enough, he left home, left Dad's church, and picked up a drug habit. It crushed my Dad. How could something like this happen? We were all raised the same way."

When it comes to parenting, one size does not fit all. Every child is unique. Do you appreciate your kids' gifts, talents, and skills? Do you really know what they are? Siblings can be as different from each other as they are from the kid next door. When parents assume their children are all the same, they can find themselves in conflict.

In this situation, the father was fortunate he did not lose all his sons. He raised them all the same way, even though they were each unique and deserved unique treatment. It turned out that Jake loved the arts, not the gridiron. He enjoyed carving up clay the way his brothers enjoyed carving up a defensive secondary. His father viewed his lack of passion for athletics as weakness, and when Jake was cut from the football team, his father accused him of not trying hard enough.

For Jake it was always the same. He never measured up to his brothers. He never pleased his father, even when his artistic talent caught the attention of others. He lived with a continual sense of rejection. And yet it turned out that he was a gifted artist living in frustration.

Jake and his dad had a clash of temperaments. They just didn't connect on a fundamental level. Jake was the square peg his dad kept trying to shove into a round hole.

While we do not believe differing temperaments *cause* rebellion, they can certainly help explain how it sometimes arises. And understanding each other's temperaments can be a great way for parents and teens to rebuild their relationship. Parenting with such knowledge can greatly reduce if not eliminate the friction that sparks conflicts. It can help prevent bad situations from getting worse and make hurting situations healthier.

Humour Me

Many good books have been written on the subject of the temperaments. *Personality Plus,* by Florence Littauer, and *How to Develop Your Child's Temperament,* by Beverely LaHaye, are two of the best. We will only scratch the surface in this discussion, so we would encourage you to pick up one of these books to gain a fuller understanding of the subject.

By *temperament* we mean a person's inborn emotional and behavioral inclinations. From the time of the early Greeks to the present, four basic temperaments (called *humours* in the Middle

Ages) have been identified: melancholy, phlegmatic, choleric, and sanguine.

Each temperament has strengths and weaknesses that contribute to or detract from healthy relationships. Melancholics are usually quiet; phlegmatics are known for their solidness; cholerics are traditionally commanding; and sanguines are often cheerful. See if you can identify in the following overview which temperaments might be living in your home.

Melancholy people tend to be quiet and serious. They are accurate, analytical, and attentive to details. The downside is that they can be highly critical of weakness or error in others. They can become so focused on details that they miss the big picture. The melancholy child is observant, withdrawn, and introspective. Her toys are neatly stacked, and her shoes are in their proper place. This child will not want to do things unless she has a fairly good chance of being successful. The melancholy parent strives for excellence, enjoys talking about theories, and wants things done "right." This parent needs to be sure he's finding things to praise about his children and is not always pointing out places where improvement is needed.

Phlegmatic folks are patient, calm, and easygoing. They are team players concerned about pleasing others. But their primary characteristic is their stability. Their consistency can be the anchor that the more flighty temperaments depend upon in relational storms. The phlegmatic child is friendly and content. However, he dislikes change, confusion, and crisis. This child is more sensitive to family instability than other children. The phlegmatic parent creates a warm, supportive home environment centered on people and routines. He remembers everyone's birthday. Because he dislikes conflict, he may tend to be overly tolerant of his children's misbehavior.

Choleric types are independent, confident, and dominant. They are natural leaders, but they can also be impatient, insensitive, and overpowering. The choleric child is often a "determined child" who will run the household if allowed to do so. This child moves from project to project, working hard but never quite finding the initiative to finish. The choleric parent is a very responsible, big picture type of person. He can become frustrated over the smallest things and sometimes enjoys projects more than people. This parent needs to guard against using anger or intimidation to attempt to control a child's behavior.

Sanguine people are fun loving, people oriented, and full of energy. They are loving and enthusiastic, the life of the party. The sanguine's greatest fear is not being accepted. The sanguine child is bright and cheerful, full of hugs, and always happy to see you, but she can find it difficult to sit still and focus. This child is highly vulnerable to peer pressure. She also needs lots of physical attention: hugs, kisses, and wrestling with Dad. The sanguine parent makes life exciting for kids. He is very good at affirming his children's strengths. But he can tend to turn a blind eye to misbehavior or even place improper weight on the child's wrong behavior.

Temperament Tantrums

Did you see some familiar traits in this review? Based on the description above, try to categorize yourself and each family member.

Tension naturally occurs when certain temperaments collide.

What happens when a melancholy mom gives birth to a sanguine son? Or when a choleric father goes toe-to-toe with an equally stubborn choleric daughter? The melancholy child will retreat under threat from Mom or Dad; the choleric will figure out a way to get even; the sanguine will try to be cute; and the phlegmatic will smile on the outside and rebel on the inside.

Understanding your family's temperaments can help bring harmony to your home. When you come to appreciate your teen's temperament and your own, you will be certain that you are parenting according to his or her uniqueness. It may be that your square peg child just needs a square hole. By understanding temperaments, you can provide just that.

CONTRIBUTING FACTOR FIVE: UNHEALTHY RELATIONSHIPS

When Mike and Patty took their daughter Megan to counseling, they thought the issues were schoolwork, choice of friends, and broken family rules. After a few preliminary sessions of airing grievances, the counselor began to ask *why* questions. Time after time, Megan shrugged and answered, "I don't know."

Mike and Patty stepped in every time, suggesting possible reasons for Megan's behavior: "She grew so fast and always looked older than her age. She's not like our other daughter; Megan's always had an independent streak."

In the middle of her parents' speculation, Megan burst out, "What do you expect? Chrissy has always been your favorite. I was always the 'big girl,' the one who was to blame."

Their daughter's revelation stunned Mike and Patty. They loved both their girls. For the rest of the day, their minds ran reruns of the past. As they thought back upon their behavior, the truth became clear. Somehow in their delight with their mild-tempered, golden-haired second daughter, they'd neglected their older one.

Parents are heroic figures. They strive to make a living for their children, to make a happy home, to raise their children well, to equip them for life. They are the single most powerful influence on their children, and they know it. They take their responsibility seriously.

But try as we might, sometimes we parents don't always do the right thing. The stresses on us sometimes bear down too much. Issues from our own childhoods sometimes interfere. Perhaps we had poor models for parenting. The love is there. The intentions are there. But sometimes we can miss the key thing our teenagers need.

There's no condemnation necessary. There's enough hurt already without anyone pointing fingers. We're bruised and beaten down. Our families may be in a mess, but we're at a loss as to how to set things right. Despite our best efforts, we may have extremely unhealthy relationships with our teenagers.

Teens will want to distance themselves from injurious family relationships. Perhaps they are presented with overly strict confinement on one hand or too lax boundaries on the other; perhaps house rules are required for the kids but not for the parents; perhaps parents have been less than honest; perhaps the parents' marriage is in a state of turmoil. If those conditions are true in a home, very often a teen will seek to break ties with the family. The teen may set himself against his parents, their ideals, and their values— i.e., he rebels—simply as a means of psychological survival. He wants to distance himself from the hurt.

The good news is that this condition can be turned around. Mistakes can be undone or atoned for. Like the computer at the beginning of this chapter, even the unhealthiest relationship can be reset and the system begun afresh. The rest of this book is dedicated to that objective.

At the Family Clinic

Children naturally desire to love and be loved by their parents above all other humans. Mom and Dad are…well…his mother and father figures. By their actions parents show the child what it's like to live in this world and whether it's a trustworthy place or not. All babies love their mothers, and all young children desire to be loved by their fathers. Parents are the ones they look to for instructions about life and encouragement about them as individuals. Children are parents' to lose.

It's the old analogy of a child as a lump of clay, longing to take the shape the parents give and trusting them to mold him in love. But sometimes the shape parents give doesn't end up being the best.

Perhaps a parent doesn't know how to parent, having never done it before or having had poor models. Sometimes one or both parents are absent. Financial stresses can be so severe that things can get out of hand at home. And so the child suffers.

Parents literally have the power of life and death over their children—emotional life as well as physical. Only parents have so much influence in the life of a child for good or ill.

A family with strong relationships can withstand whatever attacks a society hostile to happy parent/teen relations can throw at it. All the many forces arrayed against that family cannot prevail if the parents reward the trust their children naturally want to lavish on them. By the same token, a family with unhealthy relationships will have little hope of withstanding the culture's onslaught. Those external forces will shred that family like a scarecrow in a tornado.

Chapter 4 will discuss the damage parents can unintentionally do to their relationship with their teens and what to do about it. Chapter 5 will talk about building a solid family structure—rebooting the machine. The rest of the book will show you how to build a relationship with your teen that will last a lifetime.

DO THE MATH

All these factors do add up. One or more of them may be affecting your teen. Conflicting temperaments play a part. Divorce doesn't do anyone any favors when it comes to relating to teens. Nor is the society in which we find ourselves conducive to happy parent/teen relationships. And sometimes even the best-intentioned parent can find that he or she has contributed to the situation. Put all these influences together, and you can get a fatal system error—all-out rebellion—in a hurry.

There is this expectation that all teens will rebel, and so society mobilizes to make the expectation become reality in every home. We get it through media; we get it through the community; we get it through the philosophy subtly behind it all. In short, we can feel that our mental image of a happy home with teenagers in it is simply unrealistic. Might as well dream of becoming Queen of England.

Yet despite all the many contributing factors that make rebellion more likely, we continue to assert one thing: Defiance is not a pre-destined component of adolescence.

SUMMARY

The Ezzos met with Carolyn in a restaurant in Los Angeles. She was a delightful, beautiful teenager. A true joy to be around. She was very open about the problems with her parents and about her lifestyle choices.

"What do you see as the main problem, Carolyn?" Gary asked.

"My parents don't have a clue who I am."

"Why do you say that?"

"They're rich. You knew that, right? They send me all these expensive gifts, thinking that will make me be a good girl."

"You don't want what they buy you?" Anne Marie asked.

"No! Why do they have to throw that stuff at me? All they're trying to do is buy my good behavior or buy my love. I don't want any of it."

"What do you want, Carolyn?" Gary asked.

Tears rolled down both the teen's cheeks at once, as if whatever had been holding them back had been suddenly removed. "I just want *them!* Time with them. Why do they have to fly me off to the Caribbean or Japan when all I want is to be with them? Why can't we stay at home and just be *together?* We can sit on the couch or go for a walk or just stare at each other. Isn't that what families are supposed to do: be together?"

The next day, the Ezzos contacted Carolyn's parents and told them what their daughter had said. They refused to believe it.

"Our daughter loves the gifts we send. That's her love language: gift giving."

"Maybe it is," Gary said, "but right now she doesn't want your things. The gift she's crying out for is *you*. Time with you. Your attention. I can't say for sure, but I'm willing to guess that if you just brought her home, cancelled all your trips and appointments, and did nothing but spend a month of quality time with your little girl, all of her defiant behavior would begin to stop."

That's what they did, and that's what happened. Now, years later, Carolyn is completely reformed. She is happily married and at peace with herself and her parents.

Despite our best efforts, we parents can sometimes find ourselves in conflict with our teens. The liberating thing is that we can always start over. Begin today to rebuild your relationship with your teenager. The rest of this book will show you how.

BRINGING IT HOME

1. What do you think is the most significant contributing factor to teenage rebellion?
2. What are some contributing factors that weren't mentioned?
3. Is your family part of a moral community right now? If not, do you know of one you might be able to connect with?
4. Do you agree that media can feed relational tension between parents and teens? If not, why?
5. Were you able to identify your temperament and your family members' temperaments from the overview? In what way might this information help in your family?

1. For some astounding statistics about the impact divorce and absent fathers have on children, read David Blankenhorn's book, *Fatherless America: Confronting Our Most Urgent Social Problem* (New York: Harperperennial Library, 1996).

2. Art Levin, "The Second time Around: Realtities of Remarriage," *U.S. News and World Report,* 29 January 1990, 50.

SECTION TWO

GETTING BACK
ON TRACK

Starting with Moi

*D*oc," the patient said, banging his head against the wall, "it hurts when I do this."

Ever feel like that with your teenager? Sometimes parents can unknowingly bring about the very pain they receive from their teens.

When we find out we're causing ourselves or our families pain, the first thing we should do is simply stop causing more pain. This chapter will be a self-check for you as a parent to expose damage you may be doing to your relationship with your teen. If you find you've done some of these in the past, our suggestions should help you begin the healing process.

Once the patient stops causing further injury, everybody can start working on how to get to full health. That's what the following chapter and really every chapter after that is all about.

But first, let's make sure we follow the advice the head-banger's doctor gives him: "Well, you can start by not hitting your head against the wall anymore."

YOU CAN GET THERE FROM HERE

Practically speaking, where should you begin? How do you go about mending relationship bridges that have been badly damaged? How do you change old habits of parenting this late in the game? How can you bring about positive moral changes, not just outward ones that placate you, but ones within your teen's heart?

The first step is often the most difficult of the entire journey. Perhaps you made attempts in the past to reform your teen. Maybe you've tried discipline, grounding, rewards, the hard sell, the soft sell, sports, family counseling—and still there has been no improvement. Your efforts have resulted only in pain. You feel worried, helpless, hopeless, humiliated, and guilty. When the realization finally hits that you can't control your teen, despite all your efforts, you feel utterly defeated. Your relationship hurts, and you're discouraged. Can you really move from a negative to a positive relationship at this point?

We are convinced that when you make a sincere and sustained effort to change yourself first, other positive changes will occur. But it must start with you, the parent. You must be the initiator. Work to increase your influence. Become credible in the eyes of your teen. Do whatever is required to demonstrate your desire to change the status quo.

Learning how to manage your teen is secondary to learning how to lead your teen by your relational influence. That means you must take the lead in this quest and not give up. We'll deal with behavior management in later chapters, but for now the goal is to build your credibility so you can lead by your influence rather than by laying down the law.

The rest of this chapter contains suggestions for helping you get started. Applying these suggestions now can help minimize further erosion, while creating a positive change in your relationship with your teen.

PAY ATTENTION TO YOUR SPOUSE

It might seem strange to begin a chapter on restoring your relationship with your teenager by talking about nurturing a marriage, but believe us, it belongs here. Children of all ages desire their parents to live together in happy matrimony. Though there are those who will dispute this, we believe that children need a father and a mother, all living together in relative harmony, in order for the children to be psychologically healthy.

We know, however, that this may not be possible in your case. Death, divorce, remarriage, desertion, chronic illness, and a hundred other factors can cause a family to be other than the ideal. As we've said, children of divorce usually desire their parents to reconcile. There is a connection between members of a biological family that a stepparent can't fully share. A part of them will always want Dad even though such an arrangement might not be possible or even desirable.

We want to speak to parents who are married (or remarried). For the sake of your teenagers, examine your marriage's strengths. In the next chapter we'll talk about ways to make your marriage even more wonderful, but here we're talking about how to be sure you're not doing new damage. If you're together in a marriage, work on your husband/wife relationship, not just on your role as a mom or dad.

If the husband/wife relationship is not healthy, a teen has no basis for investing emotionally in the family. If the two people leading the family can't get along or if they fail to spend time alone together, family renewal can hardly be expected.

Roger and Kim's thirteen-year-old son, Neil, demonstrated this. As a youth, Neil was out of control and troublesome. It was at a point of desperation that Roger and Kim sought help through one of our videotaped parenting classes. Because Neil could not be trusted to stay home alone and no one volunteered to watch him, they brought him to the church and sat him in back of the auditorium.

In session three, the topic centered on the husband/wife relationship and the inherent need for children to know concretely that Mom and Dad love each other. That week's homework assignment directed parents to take fifteen minutes a day, when Dad or Mom comes home from work, and sit on the couch as a couple and talk. Such a simple task, repeated daily, demonstrates to children Mom and Dad's commitment to one another, which, in turn, communicates that their world is secure.

Neil's parents neglected their assignment for four days. Finally, in a moment of crisis, Neil charged his parents with not loving him. "Why can't you give me what I really need? Why can't the two of you just sit on the couch and show me that you love each other. In three weeks you haven't done anything that man on the video said to do."

Apparently, Neil was doing more than sitting in the back of the auditorium reading his biker magazine. Out of his own desperation, he was listening to every word of the presentation, hoping for change.

It never occurred to Roger and Kim that even Neil understood what they didn't: Good marriages make for good parents. More than anything else they could do or say, their son wanted to know, "Do you love each other, Mom and Dad?" From that moment on, his parents started to really love him by demonstrating their love for each other.

After that, Neil was a changed young man. According to his teachers, Neil's open opposition to authority, his anger, and his indifference to life drastically diminished. As one teacher put it, "The old Neil was drained out of his body, and a new Neil was pumped back in."

It was the same Neil, just with new hope. A secret longing of his heart was finally being satisfied. He was no longer Robert and Kim's "rebellious" son; he was now just Neil, a teenager whose heart was confident that Mom and Dad loved each other.

Every step taken to improve your marriage is a step toward strengthening your parent/child relationship, regardless of the age of your child. As you eliminate conflict in marriage, you eliminate conflict in parenting.

A beautiful marriage makes your family something worth belonging to.

ENCOURAGE YOUR TEEN

Have you ever caught yourself putting your child down? Just a small comment, perhaps not even heard. But a put-down all the same. Or maybe the praise you gave was qualified: "Great to see you've finally gotten your act together." Has there been a harshness in your tone, perhaps because you're still wounded over something he or she said previously?

How much better to let your praise be pure: "Thanks for

always remembering to close the screen door when you go through."

"I love how you help your younger sister understand things."

"I respect your opinion, especially when it comes to...."

Though teens can make parents feel as if they are utterly powerless, it isn't true. Parents have more impact on their children than any other force. It might not feel like you're having any effect on your teen, much less wounding his or her heart, but unless your words and tone have turned that heart completely to stone, you can still cause injury.

Endeavor to become your teen's greatest, most genuine, fan. A child will always welcome heartfelt support and encouragement from his or her parents. Develop a lifestyle of encouragement. There is a big difference between uttering an occasional encouraging remark and being an encouraging parent. Real encouragement flows out of a relationship. It's more than a word now and then. It's your very presence, smile, and expression that communicates encouragement.

We realize that it is easy to encourage a friend but much harder to encourage someone with whom you're in conflict. The words tend to hang in your mind, never making the final journey through your vocal chords. When words do come, they somehow are transformed into snide remarks like, "You're not as grown-up as you think," or "Don't forget you are still under my authority as long as you live here."

Check your words before they come out. Preview them. Edit out anything that feels like a put-down, and replace it with genuine encouragement.

There are many ways of delivering encouragement. You can take a moment to touch his shoulder and speak from your heart. You can write a little note for her to find in her purse. You can write a letter for his birthday, going on at length about what you love about him. Surely you can think of creative ways to do this for your teen. (See chapter 8 for how to give encouragement in a language your teen can understand.)

No matter what style of communication you choose, take your teen's need for encouragement seriously. Don't wait for warning signs to tell you how much she needs you. On the surface, it may seem as though nothing in particular is claiming her attention. Or she may be dealing with issues that seem trivial. Sometimes, to a teen in the midst of a trial, struggles that remain unspoken or are barely hinted at can be serious business. Many times parents underestimate a teen's plea. Problems which appear unimportant to us may seem insurmountable to them.

If you find you've gotten into a habit of putting your teen down, your sudden shift to words of encouragement may catch your child off guard. He may not believe you at first. Just be aware of this possible reaction. Be ready for it. But don't let it discourage you. There may be years of hurt to overcome, and both sides will find it easier to slip back into the old ways. Persevere. Keep your eye on the goal. Your sincerity and endurance will pay off in the end.

Listen for cues and realize there will be some matters of major importance couched in insignificant sounding statements. By listening carefully, you may be able to pick up on a serious problem with a friend, teacher, or foe. Or you may get wind of a problem involving peer pressure and your child. Seize these opportunities to encourage your teen through his difficulties by imparting your experience and wisdom. He needs your help and encouragement, whether he admits that to you or not.

EXPECT YOUR TEEN TO LISTEN

Does your teenager listen to you when you talk? If not, why not? Do you listen to her? Do you talk to her? Might you have fallen into a habit of what might almost be called nagging? Or perhaps you've heard from "everyone" that teenagers just don't listen to their parents, so you assume yours won't either. We've heard some parents talk about their teens' shut ears almost proudly, as if it's a mark of membership into some kind of martyred mothers club. We assure you, this doesn't have to be.

Nothing makes a teen tune out faster than constantly "reminding" her about faults or responsibilities. Homework and chores are often a case in point. "Is your homework done? Your math grade is slipping. You need to discipline yourself. This is your responsibility...."

By the third lecture your son or daughter knows what you're going to say even if you phrase it differently. They stop listening. We need to communicate effectively in order to teach the values governing personal responsibility, but nagging is not an effective training method. It won't work on your spouse, and it is even less effective on teenagers.

Another reason teens may not listen is that parents may not expect them to. Parents sometimes expect too little out of the relationship with their teen. They think it's normal for teenagers to be in constant conflict with them and that not talking and not listening are inevitable parts of adolescent behavior.

Our society expects teens to resist parental leadership and defy any infringement on the teen's autonomy. Instead of promoting the idea that great relationships can be had with our teenage sons and daughters, we are faced with a nightmarish stereotype of parents pitted against teens in a lose-lose contest of wills.

When we adopt any or all of society's expectations, it affects our parenting. We set rules and say things based more on a stereotype than on who our teen actually is. What will this do but cause him or her not to talk or listen to what we say? And the more powerless we feel to direct our child's life, the greater the tendency we feel to try to control rather than lead. So the relational cycle spirals downward to the point where there is no talking and no listening.

However, the reverse can also be true. Parenting to the true nature of your teen can promote talking and listening. When you truly get to know someone and expect his or her best, your efforts on that person's behalf make you safe to talk with and credible to listen to. In the following chapters we will look at how to get to know your teen and how to improve two-way communication.

BE SINCERE

Sometimes teens want to distance themselves from parents because of parents' sarcasm and insincerity. In an effort to draw attention to their teen's behavior problems, some parents use sarcasm in their daily conversation as a tool of coercion.

"Sure you're eating right: Those potato chips count as a vegetable, right?"

"So, what kind of trouble did you get into at school today?"

"When you act that way, I'm surprised you have any friends at all."

Sarcasm isn't usually a good motivator. Listen for discourtesies coming out of your mouth, and crimp such talk at its source.

Sarcasm forces one of two reactions from teens: Either they counterattack with their own sarcasm, or they retreat into silence. In both cases, the result is the same—the teen stops listening.

This is a tough one to turn around, but it can be done. The first thing to do is to just stop causing additional injury. It has been well said that out of the overflow of the heart the mouth speaks, so work on the pain in your own heart that may be motivating the harsh words. The rest of this book will help you bring healing to your parent/teen relationship.

PRACTICE WHAT YOU PREACH

Probably one of the most destructive forces in parenting a teen is hypocrisy. Parental hypocrisy occurs when Mom and Dad exempt themselves from the values they require their children to uphold. A double standard becomes evident when you tell your kids never to steal, but you don't return a clerk's accidental overpayment of change. Hypocrisy breeds contempt, which leads to relationship breakdown.

To be sure, no parent is perfect. We all fail to hold to our own moral standards at times. We're all hypocrites to some degree. It's okay to fail occasionally, so long as you are pursuing adherence to the same requirements you lay on your teen.

During the early years of childhood, integrity doesn't play as large a part in parental authority. Parents tell their children not to cross the street, light a fire, let the dog run loose, or climb Daddy's ladder, even though they themselves do those very things. That's not being hypocritical because these activities have no moral dimension. In such cases, parents can rightly do what they prohibit their children from doing.

But when it comes to activities that do contain a moral dimension, no disparity should exist between what parents teach and what they do, regardless of the child's age. Moral truth does not vary with a person's age.

A wise man once said that it's the little foxes that destroy the vineyard. The little acts of hypocrisy that may have gone undetected in the early years stand out like headlights during the teen years. Parental hypocrisy dismembers the family. If you're starting over or just desiring to improve your parent/teen relationship, don't merely preach your ideals. Live them.

SAY WHAT YOU MEAN AND MEAN WHAT YOU SAY

No one respects a leader who vacillates between convictions. Wishy-washiness sends a feeling of instability down to everyone below. That's not to say that parents can't change opinions or should stick with a decision even when it's clearly wrong, but once a decision is made, parents should know their reasons why and stick to them (always remaining willing to reevaluate in light of new evidence).

Teens can sense when parents are unsure of their own beliefs or leadership decisions. Too often we get into the habit of making decisions without thinking them through. Then we start waffling,

"Well, maybe just this time...." When this happens repeatedly, teens tend to acknowledge the parent's instruction but do what they please. They stop listening because they don't believe their parents are sure of what they are saying or that they have the resolve to enforce it. This teen has greater confidence in his own ability to make decisions than in his parents'.

When parents lack conviction as to what is right and wrong, they end up second-guessing every decision. That is when your teens pick up on your indecisiveness. When you as a parent say, "If you do this disobedience, such and such consequence will happen," but you don't enforce the consequence, you're just uttering empty threats. You actually make your teen despise your leadership.

Before your teen will listen and follow your instructions, he or she needs to know you believe your own words. You can't be too tired, afraid, uncertain, or just plain numb to follow through. Followers need strong leaders. If you make a promise or a threat, be sure to follow through with it. Be a leader worth following.

EXPRESS YOUR EMOTIONS APPROPRIATELY

Some parents have damaged their relationship with their teens because they've not expressed their emotions properly. It's hard not to come home from a difficult workday and, if things are frustrating at home, blow up at those we love most. But this can make the family a place of abuse not rejuvenation and safety.

Sure, there will be days when someone in the family will be in a bad mood, not talkative, and generally unpleasant to live with. Bad days and good days visit all of us. But how are you generally characterized? How do you respond when you're angry or upset? Are you able to let the rest of the family know what you feel without saying something you'll regret later?

There is a big difference between honestly expressing your feelings and angrily venting them. Expressing feelings reflects the present state of affairs which may be quite unpleasant, and this is understandable. But venting tends to be exaggerated, explosive, and belligerent.

Children are fragile. Even hardened, rebellious teens are sensitive to outbursts of frustration or anger coming down upon them from parents. As we said in chapter 3, teens will rebel from parents who do this. Wouldn't you? If this is a problem for you, take it seriously. See a counselor. Read a good book on the subject. Join a support group. You owe it to your own blood pressure to get this under control. But more so, you owe it to your family.

When your teenager sees that you are truly safe to be around and that you won't dump things on him that belong on you, he may begin to tentatively creep back into the family.

ASK (AND GIVE) FORGIVENESS

Let's say you and your teenager have been at it for a few rounds. Both sides are hurt. Both have won a few and lost a few. Each feels the other has won far more. Even if there has been no outright conflict in your home, if there is relational tension, there is hurt. If you truly want to move toward healing, the necessary first step is forgiveness.

The typical parent can easily think of things the child has done to cause pain. But it's not so easy to look in the mirror and realize that you may have caused your share of harm. If this chapter has identified some damage that you have done to your relationship with your teen, you may be squirming in your seat a bit. Or you may be weeping. If so, that's a healthy response. But don't stop there. If you're alarmed at what you've seen in the mirror, we urge you to approach your teen to ask his or her forgiveness.

In our society, people try to get the most for the least. They try to get the other person to give up more than they have to. Perhaps it's been like that in your family. Seeking forgiveness is absolutely contrary to this attitude. You can't have a chip on your shoulder and honestly ask to be forgiven. Yet it is on the basis of this humility that the fighting can cease.

Some parents fear that if they ask forgiveness, they'll be losing the little control over their teens they feel they have left. Can you relate? Seeking out an unruly or arrogant teen for the purpose of asking forgiveness is, literally, a humbling task. But by doing so, you begin to build credibility with your angry child. Humility opens the door to leading by influence (which we'll talk more about in the next chapter). To admit wrong does not detract from a parent's authority or leadership. On the contrary, it enlarges integrity.

Your teen may be skeptical at first. Is this some new trick, some new way to gain an advantage? Especially if your relationship has been volatile, this change of approach may surprise your child. But in humbling yourself to ask forgiveness, you're not out to get anything from your child. It's not an "I said it; now you say it back" proposition. When you are truly humble, you are vulnerable. That means you may get hurt. But as you show your commitment to beginning again with your child, he will eventually realize you really meant it. Someone has to be the first to bury the hatchet. Shouldn't it be you?

Seeking forgiveness for past mistakes should not be limited to your teen. You may need to approach your spouse, too. Remember that any step you take to enhance your marriage is a step taken to improve your relationship with your children. It's easy to shift blame, to point a finger at someone and mumble, "We wouldn't have these problems if you had listened to me," or "If you were around more, things would be different."

Each parent has contributed to the present state of affairs, both positively and negatively. Each makes deposits toward healthy family advancements, and each contributes his or her share of mistakes. But blaming each other for the negative and staying silent about the positive is not going to help solve family problems. Forgiving each other will.

Confess to each other your weaknesses and your hidden patterns of fear. We encourage single parents to find a friend who can hold them accountable and encourage them along the way. Confession and forgiveness can help break detrimental patterns set in motion long ago. They afford an opportunity to start fresh. Do this for the sake of your relationships and for the sake of your children, remembering that your children will always be your children. Only death truly ends all hope for reconciliation.

Asking forgiveness has many layers and applications. You may want to ask forgiveness in a general sense as a means of starting over. This can be wonderfully liberating. You may also want to ask forgiveness for specific times when you have caused hurt. Ask your teen what things have hurt her the most. Resist the temptation to drop back into the old argument; sincerely seek forgiveness for hurting your child. Then, after you've established a foundation of forgiveness, continue to build upon it. Keep the list of things you need to ask forgiveness for short and current.

A healthy family is one in which all members know that the other members do not desire to hurt and that forgiveness flows freely in all directions. You can bring that to *your* home.

One more important point to make about forgiveness. If you and your teen have had a difficult time in your relationship, you have been hurt, too, just as surely as your teen has. You need to ask for forgiveness from your teen, as we've said. But you also need to forgive your teen.

Notice we didn't say that you need to get your teen to ask your forgiveness. He or she may never do so, but you need to grant it just the same. You will never be able to go on to full healing so long as you are clinging to bitterness, hurt, and anger. For the sake of your dreams of a happy family, let it go.

SUMMARY

How refreshing to get rid of things that may have been bringing harm to your relationship with your teen! Some of these changes won't be easy, especially where there has been much injury. Whole books have been written on each topic we covered in this chapter. We're under no illusion that you can just read a chapter or even a whole book and magically have domestic bliss.

But we do believe that a happy home—that harmonious home you desire—and friendship with your grown children are impossible dreams so long as the parent/teen relationship itself is widening the wound.

Begin with the small steps you know to take right now. The

important thing is the attitude of your heart. When your teen sees you straining to do better, you may find him or her a ready ally. The rest of this book will give you tools for building that delightful future you can imagine enjoying with your teenager.

BRINGING IT HOME

1. What is the connection between a healthy marriage and security in children?
2. Have you caught yourself saying something sarcastic or discouraging to your teen recently? What did you say?
3. List at least three reasons why teens don't listen to their parents. Have you been guilty of any of these?
4. What do the authors name as one of the most destructive forces in parenting teens?
5. What is a good example of parents sending a message of "wishy-washiness" to a teen?

Chapter Five

Basics of Good Parent/Teen Relationships

*L*et's go back to our spaceship metaphor. If you found you had a leak in your capsule, the first thing you would do is work very fast to stop it. That's the part of repairing the parent/teen relationship we talked about in the previous chapter. After you've plugged the hole, you can do a spacewalk to perform full repairs. Then you can resume your journey. Making repairs and moving forward is what we'll be talking about now.

As a parent, you are the primary shaper of your child's heart and mind. Certainly there will be difficult days to endure, failures to rise up from, and mountains to climb. Other people and forces will compete to make your teen into their image. But at the end of the day, you remain the most powerful influence on your child's life.

When there is relational tension with a child, the place to focus your work is always in the parent/teen relationship. Why? Because that's where pain is felt. All the manifestations of rebellion—the arrogant attitude, the friends who make you lock up the silver, the music you despise—are not the problem. They are symptoms of something larger. The problem is a faulty parent/child relationship. So this is where you must concentrate your efforts.

We maintain that parents of teens must stop trying to parent by flexing their authority muscles and begin guiding out of the strength of their relationship. Relinquishing control is a fearful thought to some parents. To influence this child through the bond of a pleasant relationship may sound like something reserved for Mr. Rogers's Land of Make Believe. After all, to lead a teen by the power of relationship means a decent one must exist.

It starts with you making a sincere and sustained effort to change yourself. We began that process in the previous chapter. Gradually, the changes will have a positive impact on your teen. You must be the initiator. Work to increase your influence. Become credible in the eyes of your teen. Do whatever is required to demonstrate your desire to change the status quo.

Here are specific areas to get you started. Consider each with an open heart. Applying these tools now will help minimize further erosion while effecting a positive change in your relationship with your teen.

PULL THE SHOELACE

What does making a new start look like? It looks like this: Work on leading your teen, not pushing.

We can demonstrate this principle by using a shoelace. Stretch one out on a flat surface in front of you. Make the end nearer you the "bottom" and the other end farther away the "top." Now, put your finger at the bottom of the shoelace and begin pushing toward the top. What happens? The shoelace begins to stack up in loops and tangles as you push, but it does not move forward. In fact, the more you push, the more it twists and turns, moving in every direction but the one in which you want it to go. Now take the other end of the shoelace and begin pulling. What happens? The snags unwind, and you can lead the shoelace in any direction.

So it is with your teenager. When the relationship with your teenager is attractive, leading her to respond as you'd like is simpler, but pushing by force is only going to get everybody tied up in knots.

A values-based parenting approach teaches moms and dads how to lead in such a way that their teens desire to follow. Many parents wish to move their parent/teen relationship from where it is to where it should be, but they find resistance because they are pushing from the bottom rather than leading from the top. They are attempting to force change by the power of their authority instead of leading by the power of their influence.

You correct this by enhancing your relationship with your teen and by moving away from coercive parenting. Those days are over. If you desire to move into friendship with your adult children, you can't maintain an authoritative stance over them.

MORAL CONSENSUS

Managing or mismanaging authority and influence will make all the difference as to how peaceful or turbulent the teen years will be for your family. How can parents not abuse their authority with their teens?

Authority has always been a struggle for humankind. From birth, children struggle with it. It doesn't get any easier as we grow older. Some people can't seem to live with it. Most of us understand that you can't live harmoniously without it.

Authority, when properly focused, can be a beautiful thing. In a healthy family, parents use it to guide their young children by encouragement and restraint. It is necessary because law and order are dependent on the proper administration of authority. But it can be taken to extremes: Too much authority leads to totalitarianism; insufficient authority leads to injustice and social chaos. This is true for nations as well as for families.

In societies, the amount of authority needed to govern a people depends upon the moral consensus of the people. *Moral consensus* refers to values mutually agreed upon that govern individual behavior for the common good. The more values we have in common as a community, the less need there is for government to impose social order. In contrast, the more the people's values conflict with the government's values, the more intrusive government must become to insure social harmony. The same principle is true in families.

What we are striving for in our homes is social order and unity without coercive authority, especially when there is a teenager living in the house. In order to achieve that end, we must balance the need for parental authority with our teen's growing sense of personal responsibility. The closer the family draws morally, the less there is a need for rulership by authority.

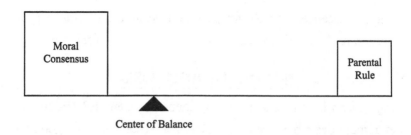

Center of Balance

Please note that the greater the moral consensus among family members, the less the need for parental rule.

The opposite effect is also possible. The less the moral consensus (that is, the greater the moral disparity between parent and teen), the more parental control must increase in order to maintain the balance of social order within the family. Whenever you increase parental controls over a teenager, you increase the likelihood of relational tension.

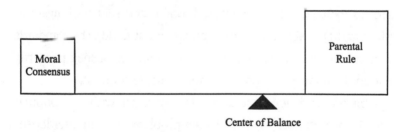

Center of Balance

Please note that the center of balance has been redefined in the second diagram. It has shifted toward more control to compensate for less moral unity. This is where all parents start out with their children, but it is not where we should be once our kids become teenagers.

Are you using more of your authority now that your children are in their teen years or less? We hope it's less. As children move into adolescence, the need for parental rule should decline in proportion to the child's increased ability to rule himself morally.

BUILD AN INTERDEPENDENT FAMILY

Is yours an interdependent or an independent family? The first is extremely desirable, even necessary. The second sounds good to those of us in the land of the free and the brave, but it is perilous. Let's look closely at each.

In interdependent families, each member is mutually dependent upon the others. Picture the two-by-fours in the frame of a house: Each individual part supports the others in order to create a whole.

A group of people holding hands and facing inward in a circle is a symbolic illustration of an interdependent family. Family values are communicated and demonstrated by Mom and Dad. They're sent to the teens, shared with each other, and sent back again to Mom and Dad, refined. In an interdependent family, the standards of moral conduct for each family member are established primarily within the home (as opposed to from outside sources).

Interdependency should not be confused with the popular counseling term *codependency*. When problems arise in interdependent relationships, the issue is confronted right then, and each individual seeks to restore the whole. When problems arise in codependent relationships, fear and insecurity produce behavior that covers up the issue and functions around it.

Interdependent families have a *team* sense about them, an ongoing loyalty to all the members. The children enjoy their parents and siblings, and the parents enjoy spending time at home with the kids. The interdependent family is not afraid to touch and hold one another publicly. Holding hands or an arm over the shoulder are signs of healthy relationships. In an interdependent family, there is a healthy concern for the welfare of the family unit and a mutual commitment to its common good.

An interdependent family provides satisfaction, protection, and security in a child's early years. It also serves as a barrier against intrusive values, especially during adolescence. The interdependent family cultivates a sense of belonging which leads to allegiance to one another and to the core values of the family. Teens grow with a "we-ism" attitude regarding their family.

Independence Day

In contrast, an *independent* family structure leads to "me-ism." Such a family is free from influence, guidance, or the control of another. That sounds attractive to our American sensibilities—didn't we fight for our independence? But what it means in a family is that individual family members are unaffiliated, alienated, and not committed to one another.

Members of independent families are simply not on the same page with one another. There is an unhealthy sense of self-reliance in these homes. There is no consistent feeling of belonging because there is no sense of needing to belong. Relationships are independent and becoming more so. The more independent they become, the more distant family members are from one another. Do you know someone who gives up on relationships or loyalties and turns to new ones overnight? This flippant view of commitment may be the fruit of an independent family.

The independent family symbolically holds hands and stands in a circle, too. But instead of all members looking in toward one another, each member looks out, away from the center. They look unified from a distance, but it is far from being what it should be. Everyone is caught up in his own little world, doing his own independent thing.

As a result, teens from independent families turn to their peers for support, love, and values. They do it not so much out of bald-faced rebellion as from the fact that they're just not getting them at home. It is the nature of independence to breed isolation, not camaraderie. When problems come, the teens turn outward to their peers, not inward to their family.

The independent family fails to provide the opportunities that normally bring families together. Meals, bedtime, and family activities give opportunities to regroup and engage in meaningful conversation. But if you don't provide the opportunities for talk, talk doesn't happen. Family members stand alone, even in a crowded house.

Choosing Interdependence

On paper, most people would choose the interdependent family structure. Everyone wants to belong, to be loved, and to be supported. But for the structure to work in real life, it means sacrifice. It means being there for one another.

The process begins with parents. We must be there for our family. There will always be better jobs, higher positions, deeper classes, more convenient gyms, and greater opportunities for enrichment. These are all good, and it is hard to say no to them. But when parents no longer make time to fulfill their role as the primary moral influence over their teens, the resulting vacuum will eagerly be filled by other influences: media, public institutions, and peers. Those voices are often opposed to your goal of family harmony. The result can be nothing but increased alienation, indifference, and independence on the part of your teens.

Building an interdependent family takes intentionality; it certainly won't come about by accident. The natural tendency is for family members to fly outward from the center like marbles on a merry-go-round. But the way to achieve interdependency is to create reasons for the marbles to stay put. (More on how to do this in chapter 7.)

NURTURE YOUR MARRIAGE

In chapter 4 we talked about marriage from an almost negative stance: why it's important not to neglect your marriage. Here are a few ideas from the positive side to help make your marriage a thing of beauty.

Date Night

Do your teens ever see you arm-in-arm with your spouse? Do you ever tell them you'll be with them in a few minutes, after you and your spouse have had time to talk? Do you and your spouse ever go on dates together—even weekends or longer away?

Your teenagers need to see that your marriage is important. They may protest when they can't have the car because you two are going out, but your commitment to the marriage will send a wonderful message. It tells them their world is stable. All is right with the universe. "Mom and Dad love each other. I'm going to be okay." It speaks to them on a subconscious level.

Start and maintain a regular date night with your spouse.

Couch Time

In *Childwise* and *Preteen Wise,* we talk about "couch time." This is time in which Mom and Dad sit together, while the children are *awake* and in the house, and simply talk together about their day. The children are welcome in the room but not in the conversation (nor on the couch). They need to see in a tangible way that your spouse comes first for you—even before them.

Young children may whine or cry to try to get your attention back on them. Teens may crank up the TV. But you have to resist their efforts. In time, if you persevere, they will grow to welcome your couch time. Sometimes children will even remind their parents to have that time if they've forgotten. Couch time is another way to send the message to children that their world is stable.

Now, if your teen doesn't know you're having couch time, it won't work. You and your spouse may be sitting on the couch all day long, but if she's locked in her room with the music at one hundred decibels, the effect will be lost on her. The principle of couch time, though, remains important, even for teens. They still need to know their parents value their marriage above all else.

A teenager from a stable home will be less likely to rebel than a teenager from a broken home, an angry home, or even just a home in which Mom and Dad's love for each other is doubtful. Show your teens your commitment to the marriage. They will interpret it as commitment to them.

GET TO KNOW YOUR TEEN

What makes your teen tick? What is his particular giftedness? What are her favorite pastimes? Does he like computers, sports, classical music, or the hum of a high-powered engine? You must become a student of your teen.

Learn to ask open-ended questions that require a thoughtful response. Rather than asking, "How is school going?" to which your child can reply "Fine," try digging a little deeper:

"What's the hardest part about your new math class?"

"What do you think are the most important qualities in a friend?"

"If you could go absolutely anywhere for a vacation, where would you go?"

"What would you want people to say about you at your funeral?"

Such information is too valuable to waste.

When a distant acquaintance calls us by name, we're impressed. When someone takes the time to get to know us, we're appreciative. When someone engages in the give and take necessary to truly understand us, we're friends for life. We feel valued, worth knowing.

So it is with your teen. Pursue her. Ask his opinion. Study her. Go spelunking in his personality. Be willing to learn new things and appreciate new tastes. You may find you already have your best friend right in your own home.

REALLY LISTEN TO YOUR TEEN

You can start learning about your teenager simply by listening to him. Really listening.

Sometimes kids can get the impression that it is never the "right time" to talk with their parents. Maybe they think they'll never get Mom and Dad's undivided attention during a conversation.

We all know how irritating it is to talk to someone who isn't interested enough in what we're saying to be all ears. It sends the message that not only is our topic not interesting, but *we* are not worth listening to. Most of us will simply write that person off as someone who's too self-important to bother with.

Parents don't intend to send the message that they're unavailable or only half-listening, but they frequently do. Preoccupation with jobs, yard work, other kids, and even hobbies can leave a teen feeling like everything else is more important than he is. Sharing Dad or Mom's attention with the newspaper, TV, computer, or grocery list is both a put-off and a put-down.

There will be times when you can't talk "right now." But it's important to make time to do so as soon as you can. During those times when you do talk, do you listen fully and with focused attention? Listening with your eyes is as much part of the conversation as listening with your ears. If your eyes keep drifting to the TV, you're only half listening, if that. Teens are acutely sensitive to this.

In such cases, not communicating at all produces less frustration for teens than talking to a parent who only half listens. This is not hormone-induced rebellion! It's a decision grounded in mature reasoning: "They don't listen when I talk, so why waste my breath?" You'd do the same.

Be sure you're not answering before they finish talking either. Gary admits to having failed his own children this way on a number of occasions. There were times when he thought he knew where a conversation was headed and jumped in with both feet, only to realize later that he'd been wrong.

Like many fathers, he listened only long enough to get what he thought was the gist of what his child had to say and then quickly offered a solution: "Okay, this is what you need to do." Perhaps in an effort to appear decisive and wise, a parent, especially a dad, can sometimes race to the first set of steps that would solve the problem (the problem the parent *thinks* the teen is talking about). Consequently you can come up with a perfectly sensible solution to a problem your teen is not having. Would you keep asking advice of someone who did this?

Sometimes teens need to talk things through. Just because your teen comes to you with a problem doesn't mean she's looking for a solution. This is a hard lesson for some of us dads to learn. We want to fix whatever's broken. But often the best help you can offer your teenager is to just play counselor: listen, rephrase ("What I hear you saying is that..."), and empathize. It's amazing how sometimes we can find our own solutions simply by listening to ourselves talk to someone else about the problem.

On one occasion, Gary's daughter Amy confided to him that she had no close friends. Gary responded instantly, "Of course you do. Don't be silly!" Although he was trying to sound encouraging, he actually cut her communication short. He listened to her words but not to her feelings. Later that evening, Gary's wife, Anne Marie, informed him of a struggle Amy was having with a close friend. In this case, Anne Marie had responded by listening to the deeper message. She listened between the lines rather than reacting only to the words.

Listening with focus. That's all your teen wants from you when she's talking. With the simple act of muting the TV (or better yet, turning it off) and turning in your chair to face her, you tell her that she's valuable to you—even more important to you than *Monday Night Football* or *Days of Our Lives.*

REALLY TALK TO YOUR TEEN

The corollary to really listening to your teen is really talking to her. Some parents only engage in shallow, "How was your day?" talk. Once again, it may stem from a subconscious feeling on parents' parts that they've got more important things to get to, or perhaps they've believed the hype that says teens don't really want to talk to "old" people.

When you're having a conversation with your teen, be sure to go beyond exchanging facts or giving instructions and correction. This is the lowest level of communication and sometimes occurs when parents are satisfied merely to receive or give data. This may be due to the busyness of the day, the rush to get dinner on the table, or the desire to head out the door for a meeting or event. This can develop if there tends to be conflict between a parent and a teen: Better to keep it shallow than get the unending fight going again.

Communication will not improve so long as the parent is satisfied to let it remain at this level. If there is parent/teen conflict, it certainly won't evaporate based on an absence of words.

Now, to be sure, gathering facts pertaining to your child's day is important. Some small talk is necessary. But if that is the only level on which you communicate, don't be surprised if you get this type of exchange:

"How was your day?"

"Okay."

"How did you do on your quiz today?"

"I dunno."

"Where are you going tonight?"

"Out."

"Out where?"

"I dunno."

"Do you know when you're coming home?"

"Nope."

Real heart-to-heart stuff, huh? Which came first, the shallow conversation or the shallow relationship?

Turn off the television. Skip going to the gym one time. Take your teen with you to get a milkshake. Go somewhere where you can really engage in conversation. If you have conflict to work out, this would be a good time to do it. But if things seem to be going along fine, make the effort to find out what's really going on in his life.

Your teen will detect how genuine your interest is, so be sincere. If this is a new thing, or if there is much hurt or a confirmed pattern of rebellion, she may push you away at first. But pursue. Don't take the hurt, and don't go quietly. If you maintain sincere interest in your child's world—whether it means going to every game, concert, play, debate, or whatever else—you will begin to reap the dividends.

Plan Heart-to-Hearts

Talking and listening are vital parts of any healthy relationship. Without them, relationships wither as surely as plants without water. It's best to schedule regular opportunities for these dialogues rather than waiting for problems to indicate the need for them. Don't rely upon chance meeting times to hear from your teens. Plan those times; make opportunities.

Outside activities can provide great occasions for communication. Go for a walk with her; go to a ball game; go out for a morning stroll through the mall; take him fishing or boating or on a long bike ride together. Before you can have heart-to-heart conversations, you have to be in close proximity. Every opportunity to talk won't result in a deep conversation, but it's important that you provide the opportunities just the same. You never know when your teen's got something on her heart she'd really like to talk to you about.

In the Ezzo household the primary time for heart-to-hearts was at bedtime. They had an interesting arrangement. Some nights the girls sat on the edge of Mom and Dad's bed, tucking their mother and father in while recounting the day's activities. The next night it was Mom and Dad's turn to sit on the edge of their children's beds and talk.

Those nightly efforts accomplished more than simply providing a chance to talk. They provided a necessary opportunity to care for the family at a deeper level of communion. All those nights spent sitting on each other's beds, listening to one another, and participating in meaningful conversation touched each person on a deep level.

When talk time doesn't take place for one reason or another, there will be much discontent and loneliness among family members. Some families don't know what they don't have. They don't realize the value of making opportunities to develop the soul of the family—until they no longer have it.

Consciously set up times when you and your teen can be alone together. Maybe a trip to the neighboring city, maybe a girls' night at home, maybe a walk by the beach. Provide the opportunity and see what happens.

WORK THROUGH YOUR CONFLICTS

All families have conflict. Stress, trials, conflicts, financial problems, and selfish attitudes beset healthy families as much as they do unhealthy ones. The difference is that healthy families are committed to working through their conflict.

It's so easy to look for the exit when problems come, thinking that this group of humans was just somehow defective and surely another set would be superior. Teens are as guilty of this as adults. But it's safe to say that all people have problems, and all families will have hard times. There's an old song that says, "You can run to the end of the highway, but your feet won't make your troubles disappear." If you're going to have stress wherever you go, you might as well stay where you are and get busy working through it.

In stress-filled families, conversations can quickly flare up into arguments. As a result, both parents and teens tend to pull away from each other, silently agreeing that it is preferable not to talk than to openly wage war. But silence is unnatural in a family, as it is in marriages. To be silent is to be in control, even when emotions are raging just below the surface.

Determine to resolve conflict instead of avoiding it. Learn to draw upon one another's strengths to get through these trials. Confess your faults to each other. Seek and grant forgiveness. Remember that what you're fighting for is worth any amount of struggle to achieve. Take the hard way, the heroic way, and work it out.

SUMMARY

We are now at the end of our section on getting the family's spaceship turned around. We've assessed the damage; we're working on preventing further injury to the capsule; and we are now back on course toward earth. For the remainder of *On Becoming Teenwise,* we'll be talking about how to maximize speed, avoid turbulence, and enhance crew enjoyment.

The main task now will be to give your teen reasons to invest in the family. Your goal will be to make the family the place of comfort, of belonging, and of friendship for every member. When people make investments into something, they take an acute interest in it. They watch it; they follow its progress; and they work for its success.

BRINGING IT HOME

1. Explain the shoelace illustration in your own words.
2. What is the difference between leading by authority and leading by influence? Write down one way you can apply that to your family this week.
3. What is the difference between an independent and an interdependent family?
4. What is couch time, and what message does it send to teens?
5. What do the authors mean when they talk about *focused attention?*

Chapter Six

Principles of Correction

When an airliner takes off, the flight engineer determines what direction the pilot needs to steer the plane to get on the desired course. Sometimes the plane gets off that course. When that happens, it's up to the air traffic controllers in the control towers to highlight that and give instructions to get back on course.

So it is with teenagers: Sometimes they get off course. It falls to parents to make sure they can find their way back to the right path.

When a teenager needs correction, it's not something parents go into with the intent to hurt or punish, with no other goal but to cause pain. It's something they do out of love to be sure their teen gets to the right destination. Parents use as much correction as is necessary to realign the teen's course, but no more.

In this chapter we give you principles that will help you on those occasions when your teenager really does need to be corrected. These are tools that have been proven effective in thousands of homes very much like yours. The Nathan parable, especially, is great for those times when your teen may not realize what she's doing is wrong. We'll start with what we call the five laws of correction.

THE FIVE LAWS OF CORRECTION

As we have said, by the time a child is in his teens, you should be leading less through the exercise of your authority. Therefore we will only present the laws in summary form. If you're interested in the fuller treatment, we recommend you pick up one of our earlier books, especially *On Becoming Childwise*.

First Law of Correction: Distinguish between Mistakes and Defiance

There is a distinction between the fifteen-year-old who accidentally crushes his brother's new CD and the teen who goes on a rampage because he wasn't invited to the beach with his brother's friends. When you're deciding the proper means of correction for a situation, be sure to determine whether the deed was done out of innocence or malice.

In our previous books, we referred to innocent disobedience as *childishness*. It's when the young person does something wrong but wouldn't have if he had known it was wrong or had been able to prevent it. *Defiance,* on the other hand, refers to those acts that are done intentionally to cause injury or loss. Childishness is usually a head problem—a lack of knowledge. Defiance is usually a heart problem—the child does not want to do right.

Parents should make the distinction between mistakes and intentional disobedience and discipline accordingly.

Second Law of Correction: All Correction Must Promote Learning

Fifteen-year-old Liz knew that only her best friend, Sue, was allowed in the house if her parents weren't home. Liz had once gotten cornered into an uncomfortable situation with too many friends over, making a mess all over the house. So, when Sue stopped over with her boyfriend, looking for a quiet place to be alone with him, Liz let both of them in. It wasn't a group, after all, just two people, and one was Sue. She figured this would be all right.

Mom and Dad, however, had strong opinions to the contrary. Apparently, their original restriction did not promote learning. Liz wasn't able to apply the past lesson to her present situation.

The goal in correction isn't merely to correct a single act of defiance but to prevent it from ever happening again. Many times this can be accomplished just by explaining why the thing was wrong. When you instill into a teen's heart the *why* of correction, you'll be far less likely to be dealing with that issue in the future. If learning did not take place, correction didn't happen.

Third Law of Correction: The Punishment Should Fit the Crime

As adults, we do not get punished by our parents for our decisions. Our punishment is that we have to live with the consequences of our choices. So should it be with your teen. When your child was young, punishments were appropriate. But when a child becomes a teenager, punishment should play a greatly diminished role. In its place, use natural and logical consequences—modified to fit the situation—to accomplish your correction.

We once heard someone teach that every disobedient act by a child should be punished the same way: by beating the child. But disobedience comes in all sizes and frequencies, so there can be no one punishment or correction that is appropriate for them all. (And children should never be beaten.)

Factors that parents should weigh when considering appropriate correction include:

- the age of the teen (Is this a child who has just entered the teen years or a seasoned veteran of seventeen?)
- the frequency of the offense (Is this the second time or the seventy-second?)
- the context of the offense (Was your child the instigator or a follower?)
- the overall characterization of the child's behavior (Is this behavior unusual or common?)
- the need for balance in discipline (Too harsh brings exasperation; too little breeds contempt)

Fourth Law of Correction: An Offense against a Person or Property Requires an Apology

Relationships work best when there is no unresolved conflict between them. If your teenager has committed an offense against someone or someone's property (but no monetary damage was done), he owes an apology.

There is a difference between giving an apology and asking for forgiveness. Either or both may be appropriate in a situation, but they are not the same. An apology is a simple, "I'm sorry." This is called for when the teenager has accidentally offended the person or abused the property or if he did so not knowing he wasn't supposed to. In this case a sincere apology is usually sufficient.

But if there was intent to harm or offend, "I'm sorry" won't cut it. Now the teenager needs to seek forgiveness. This means humbling himself before the other person, confessing what he's done, and requesting the person's forgiveness. This requires a contrite, penitent attitude—which, by the way, is a wonderful thing in anyone.

The offended party may not grant forgiveness. They may be too hurt or angry. But that's not your teen's concern. If he presents himself in humility and expresses a willingness to make it right, that's enough. America is full of bitter, unforgiving people. That's their choice. But if your teen has made a legitimate request for forgiveness, he has done what he could and should have to think about it no more.

Why is this forgiveness thing so powerful? Because when a teen merely says, "I'm sorry," she's in control of that moment. She controls the depth and sincerity of her sorrow. But when she seeks forgiveness, the one she's humbling herself before is in control. She's asking something of that person that she cannot get without his or her consent—forgiveness. It is this humbling effect that so wonderfully curbs a teen's (and a parent's) appetite for going back and doing the same wrong thing again.

Fifth Law of Correction: If Financial Liability Occurs, the Teen Should Make Restitution

In the real world, "If you broke it, you bought it." It shouldn't be any different for your teen. Mom and Dad can't come bail Junior out every time he makes a costly mess. If they do, they'll be doing it for the rest of his life. This is part of instilling into your teen responsibility for his own actions.

Parents can use restitution to teach, too. Make the level of restitution fit the crime. If the teen caused one hundred dollars damage because she accidentally knocked someone's dishes onto the floor, she should work until she could repay the one hundred dollars—or, better yet, until she could replace the dishes. If, on the other hand, she broke the dishes in a vicious tantrum, the restitution ratio should be two-to-one, three-to-one, four-to-one, or even higher. Restitution is a good teacher.

Always remember that correction is not about getting even with our teens but about teaching. The aim is to make the right path clear to your teen and, when necessary, put him back on it.

A BARREL OF MONKEYS

Sixteen-year-old Gina just can't seem to grasp the concept of rinsing off her plate and placing it in the dishwasher. Apparently she believes the burden of carrying her plate from the table to the sink is more than enough for her to bear.

Mom, on the other hand, believes Gina can do a bit more. Yet each evening, Mom watches speechlessly as Gina casually places the plate in the sink and retreats toward her room. Gina is usually halfway up the stairs before Mom's voice reaches her. "The dishwasher, Gina. That's where your dirty dishes belong." Gina stomps back down the stairs and almost breaks the plate as she shoves it into the dishwasher rack.

It's an unpleasant ritual they act out every day. Mom yearns to turn this around. But how? The answer lies not with Gina but with Mom. So long as she's always reminding Gina—and never disciplining her—the lesson will not stick. She's teaching her daughter that there really is no consequence for neglecting this chore, so why should Gina ever do it?

Parents have to transfer the responsibility for correct behavior onto their children. When a child is one, his parents do virtually everything for him. But every month and year that passes should see his parents teaching him how to do more and more himself. One of the main goals of parenting is to raise up a self-governing, conscientious young person who has internalized the responsibility for right attitudes and actions.

Excuse Me, Is This Your Monkey?

If this doesn't seem to be happening with your teen, first look to yourself. Many times, well-meaning parents can contribute to this problem by continuing to do for their children. Do you constantly remind your teen to do things you know she already knows she's supposed to do? Do you hear yourself giving the same prompting for the thirtieth time this week? If so, that's where you need to start. You need to break yourself of this habit and start enforcing penalties for your teen not heeding something she knows to do.

Until parents learn how to transfer ownership responsibility for behaviors to their children, those children have no reason to be accountable for their actions. No child will ever become self-governing so long as Mom and Dad are always prompting. With your constant reminders, you teach your teen that you aren't serious. If the command were something you really needed her to respond to, her failure to do so would create all kinds of consequences. If no consequences ever come, then no compliance will ever come either.

In Gina's case, she knew that sometimes her mom would call her back to the sink and sometimes she wouldn't. Sometimes her mom would do the chore herself. She knew she could wear her mother down. If Mom got too tired to call Gina back downstairs, so much the better. There might be a lingering sense of guilt about manipulating her mother that way, but if she could get away with it, with only the occasional lecture as punishment for disobedience, it was well worth doing.

Constantly reminding your teen to do what is expected only means you have no expectation.

When your teenager understands what he's supposed to do and that he's supposed to do it, that should be it. You shouldn't have to remind him about it. If it's a brand-new behavior and he's just not accustomed to thinking about it, then one reminder the first time might be appropriate. But anything beyond that and you risk falling into the habit of always reminding him. Unless your teen has some kind of learning disorder that prevents him from remembering, you should back off.

A parent who constantly reminds a teen to do something he's supposed to do on his own has not transferred responsibility: He's taken it back on himself. Notice that this is not the teen's problem but the parent's. If you want to bear the burden of remembering, he's usually pleased to let you do so. One less thing.

Responsibilities are like monkeys. They like to hop from one person's back to another's. Parents start out with the child's entire barrel of monkeys. As the child grows, his parents begin handing him his monkeys as he's able to take them on. By the time the child is grown, he should be carrying all his monkeys.

A parent who assigns a task, then retains the burden of remembering to do it, has allowed that monkey to jump back onto her. Send them back! Your goal is to get rid of the monkeys not collect them.

Your primary ally in this crusade is a simple little phrase: "Do you have the freedom?"

Monkey Repellent

Sixteen-year-old Jake asks to borrow the car one fine spring day. The guys are starting up a game of hoops over at the gym, he tells Mom. So, Mom thinks quick. No, she doesn't need the car, but aren't there a few things Jake needs to handle before taking off?

"What about the lawn?" she asks. "Didn't Dad say he needed your help with that this morning since company's coming this afternoon? And what about the tools you left out in the garage last night? You told Dad you'd clean them up first thing. Did you do that? Oh, and remember, when you use the car, you need to put a few dollars in the jar on the counter to help pay for gas. Do you have that right now?"

Do you hear the sound of monkeys jumping? Mom's checklist of reminders has yanked those primates straight back onto her shoulders. There's a better way for her to handle this. We call it monkey repellent.

Think of privileges as freedoms. A teen who has earned the privilege of not needing a curfew has the *freedom* to stay out late. Teens gain privileges and freedoms by rightfully carrying out chores and responsibilities. A teen who has not completed his responsibilities is not entitled to enjoy the associated level of freedom. Freedom and self-governance are connected.

Here's how Jake's mom should have answered: "Jake, I know Dad spoke with you last night about some responsibilities. Do you have the freedom to play basketball right now?"

Uh, oh. Now Jake's the one squirming. He knows his responsibilities very well, and now Mom's expecting him to be accountable for them. He may not like it, but he understands that his freedoms are contingent on his obligations. That's the way real life is, isn't it? If you don't get up and go to work every day, you don't get paid. Jake may not realize it right now, but his mom is helping him learn how to succeed in the real world.

The question, "Do you have the freedom to do that?" repels monkeys because it puts the burden of ownership back on the child. It forces him to think. *Well, do I?* Contrast that with Mom's checklist of reminders. Which one do you think will provoke a teen to greater initiative and follow-through?

An additional benefit to a teen learning how to internalize his own sense of responsibility is that he is less susceptible to peer pressure. He has learned to think about freedoms and responsibilities for himself and therefore is not dependent on others to do his thinking for him.

Monkey Business

The typical teen really does want to look you in the eye and honestly say, "Yes, Mom, I do have the freedom to shoot hoops. I took care of the chores and already put a few bills in the jar."

If a teen tells his parents that he has the freedom to do something and in reality he doesn't, consequences are necessary. Let's say Jake's jobs were not completed, but he told his mom they were just so he could get out the door. Upon his return, there would be another discussion.

Of course he would need to get busy doing the chores. But

that's not a consequence since he'd been assigned those duties in the first place. There would need to be some further penalty. Perhaps he loses the freedom of playing basketball with the guys for a month. Perhaps he loses car privileges or his open-ended curfew for a certain length of time.

Freedoms and responsibilities are connected. As you learn to pass your teen's monkeys onto him, and as your teen learns to be in charge of his own attention to those assignments, his freedoms should go up and your parent/teen relationship should soar.

SUBSTITUTION VS. SUPPRESSION

Your daughter brings home a CD with objectionable lyrics. You want to march right in there and confiscate the disc and maybe the CD player itself while you're at it. But that may not be the best way to put an end to the behavior that's bothering you.

Your son's asking for an extremely violent computer game for his birthday. It's supposed to have the most awesome graphics and gameplay on the planet, or so he says. He's played it at his buddy's house, so he knows he likes it. You go to the store and watch a demo, and you're sickened by the realistic gore you see splattered everywhere. You're so mad that you're ready to go home and say, "You want some violence? I'll give you some violence." But that might not be the most effective approach.

With teenagers (and adults, for that matter) sometimes we can't just squelch the bad behavior we want eliminated. Simply pulling the plug on an activity or forbidding a relationship may backfire: It is likely to cause the other person to rise up and fight. Then it becomes a battle of wills. You'll be tempted to exert your authority—"Because

I said so!"—causing your teen to be sorely tempted to defy you.

There's a better way. We call it using substitution over suppression. If you want to stop your teen's relationship with one group of kids, for instance, you'd better be making friends with families whose children you'd prefer your teen to be with. If you're going to ban one kind of music, do some research so you can recommend some "cool" alternatives. If you want your daughter to stop seeing that boy, maybe it's time for Daddy to come back into the picture since that's probably who she's seeking a substitute for anyway. If your teen is jealous all the time, don't just try to squelch his jealousy, teach contentment and generosity.

You can't just take away something someone cares deeply for and leave a vacuum. There has to be a substitute, something new for the person to put in its place, or he will go back to the old ways. He doesn't know any other way.

It is better to guide your teens away from behaviors and relationships of which you do not approve with substitutes than it is to try to squash those behaviors and relationships by parental decree. The beauty of the substitution method is that not only do you get your teen to stop doing the bad thing, but you have the opportunity to introduce him to something you value and esteem.

THE NATHAN PARABLE

There is an old story about King David, the second king of ancient Israel. Instead of going out with his army to campaign, he stayed at the palace—and got into trouble. As he was strolling around on the roof of his house, he saw a beautiful woman taking a bath. This was Bathsheba, the wife of one of David's loyal soldiers. David sent for her and she came. Thus began a series of events that led to adultery, deceit, and ultimately murder.

At the height of David's folly, the prophet Nathan came to him with a story. He told a tale of an injustice that had been done in David's kingdom. A very rich man, owner of great flocks, had had a visitor arrive at his home. Rather than slaughter one of his own sheep for the guest, the rich man went to his poor neighbor who had only one sheep, a little ewe who was so close to him that he slept with it, and killed that sheep for the meal.

David was furious. "Any man who would do such a thing deserves to die! He must repay four lambs to the poor man for the one he stole and for having no pity."

Then Nathan spun on him and said, "You are the man!"

He showed the king how he had defrauded and murdered Bathsheba's husband for his wife when David's own harem was overflowing. David was pierced to the heart over what he had done. Though he was never again the king he had been, at least he was rescued from complete destruction, and the throne did not pass from his family.

Nathan used a parable to get David to see something to which he'd turned a blind eye. You may find parables a powerful tool to use with your teenager. The appeal of a made-up story like this is that you can show the crucial problem in high relief, holding it up to the light for all to see, but in a nonthreatening way. It's just a story, after all. It's even better if you can get the teen to contribute to the story, saying how wrong that person in the story is. Then, when you get to the end, she has her own words to deal with.

Gary and Anne Marie Ezzo once counseled a couple who had

implied that someone was guilty of a certain offense simply based on circumstantial evidence and the fact that they didn't know the accused *hadn't* committed it. Because this couple had made similar insinuations in the past (ones that later had proven to be false), the Ezzos felt they needed to do something to help them see what they were doing.

Instead of confronting the issue head-on, when the Ezzos were with them next they set up a parable. As the unsuspecting couple listened, they began their story:

"This week our car was hit by another car."

"Oh, dear," this couple said. "Was everyone all right?"

"Yes, everyone's fine. It happened at night, while it was parked."

"That's a relief."

"Of course whoever did it drove off without leaving a note or anything. But we think we know who did it."

"How? Did someone see something?"

"No, but we can tell it was hit by a white car because there's white paint in the dent in our blue car. When we took it to the insurance company, they asked us, 'Do you know anyone who owns a white car?' And we said we did because you two own a white car, don't you?"

They didn't answer right away. "What are you saying? Are you suggesting that we hit your car and drove off?"

The Ezzos shrugged.

"Well, that's preposterous," the couple said. "I can't believe we're hearing this. We would never do something like that and then drive off."

"I know you say that, but you do have a white car, don't you?"

"Yes, but that doesn't—"

"And we don't know that you *didn't* hit our car."

"But we didn't!"

"So you say. But we went ahead and told the police that we were pretty sure it was you."

The Ezzos did eventually tell them it was only a parable, but it certainly got the point across. They were able to see with absolute clarity how they had damaged reputations and friendships by their reckless accusations.

If you suspect your teen is doing something wrong or if you want to present the dangers of something your teen is doing, consider using a Nathan parable. You can tell it as a real story, as perhaps something that happened at work today, or you can make it clear that it's just a made-up story to illustrate something.

When you come to the *You are the man* point, be sure to retain your gentleness without sacrificing your clarity. Chances are, when you take the curtain away and reveal what you've been saying, you and your teen will have some talking to do. Maybe you got something wrong, or maybe it's not the way you were thinking at all. But as long as you're talking, it's a good thing.

SUMMARY

By the time a child becomes a teenager, she's developed most of what her personality and identity are going to be. There will still be a need for correction, just as a pilot makes minute course corrections as he's flying. And there may be times when unexpected turbulence disrupts the smooth flight. But as long as you keep in mind the five laws of correction, keep the monkeys where they belong, substitute rather than suppress, and use parables, you should stay well on course and arrive at your desired destination.

BRINGING IT HOME

1. What is the primary difference between childishness and defiance?

2. Fill in the blank: "If learning did not take place, _____ didn't happen." What does this mean?

3. What is the difference between an apology and asking forgiveness? What's so powerful about seeking and granting forgiveness?

4. What is restitution, and why is it such a good teacher?

5. What is the monkey repellent phrase, and why does it work?

THOSE FANTASTIC TEEN YEARS

Chapter Seven

Courting
Family Investors

The Stedman family was a wreck. Their seventeen-year-old son, Brian, had so little respect for his parents that he was calling his real, biological, at-home dad by his first name. His choices in body art and hairstyle were shocking to his parents, and they couldn't even bring themselves to talk about his friends.

They turned to one of our teen seminars out of hopelessness. One homework assignment was to let the teen plan a family night. Brian asked if it had to be something out in public. He said he wouldn't be caught dead out somewhere with his parents. We said it didn't have to be in public, but it had to be something the teen took ownership of.

It took a week, but he finally came up with his decision, and it surprised everyone: He said he wanted to go to the mall with his parents.

In a state of disbelief, the Stedmans found themselves walking into the "in" mall with their son. Both parties had to fight the temptation to ditch who they were with. But the thing that shocked them the most was that they had a great time together. Brian had planned a trip to the food court for dinner; the arcade for a few games; a store for mom, a store for dad, and a store for him; and dessert by the fountain.

Several of Brian's friends came up and met his parents. They asked if Brian wanted to come with them to a movie. The Stedmans said he could go, but Brian said he'd rather hang with his parents.

Afterwards, Brian admitted that he had had an "acceptable" time at the mall with Mom and Dad. From that time forward, their family turned around. This family began doing more and more together, letting Brian plan his share of activities, and fundamentally rebuilding their relationship and family identity.

This can happen in your home, too.

OFF THE WALL STREET

What you invest in, you care about. Consider the stock market. The money goes in, then every day you watch the market fluctuate. The better the return, the more you are willing to invest. People tend not to walk away from an investment that cost a great deal. Having a stake in something gives us a reason to stick around—to nurture, watch, and add to our portfolio.

Or consider a boat at a dock. Sailors fasten mooring lines to cleats on the pier to keep the vessel from floating away. The ropes or cables must be tight enough to keep the boat in place, but not so tight as to prevent it from being able to adjust to the effect of the waves.

So with teenagers. The natural tendency of young people is to drift away from their moorings, their families of origin. It is the parents' task to affix mooring lines to keep them at home. Not chains of authoritative restriction, but loving ties that make teens desire to remain close: tight enough for safety, loose enough for individuality. The more reasons you give them to remain true to your family, the happier everyone will be.

You want so much from your relationship with your teens. We know your goal is more than simply to turn out okay kids who don't do drugs or crash the car headfirst into a tree. It's not just the absence of something negative (say, having a police officer regularly show up at your door with your teen in tow) that you're after, but the presence of something positive. We hope your goal is to have a child who doesn't just tolerate your family, but who loves it and serves it and contributes to it.

You want your teenagers to be investors in this venture you call a family. This chapter will give several ideas for how to form attractive ties binding the members of your family to one another.

BUILD FAMILY IDENTITY

The first step in securing teenage investors is to make the family something worth investing in. You do that by building an attractive family identity. Here's how.

Friendship with your adult children may be a parenting dividend you didn't give much thought to while you were changing diapers, giving baths, or reading bedtime stories. But as your children grow, it's important to ask: "When my children become old enough to select their own friends, will they have any reason to choose us or their sisters and brothers? Do my children consider members of their family part of their inner circle of most loyal friends?" If you have a strong family identity, the answers to these questions can be yes.

What is family identity? It's knowing who you are as a unit. All members know what the family stands for, what it won't stand for, and who they stand for: namely, one another. It's one for all and all for one. Family identity is an attitude that all members accept one another and are fiercely loyal to one another. It's an understanding of that family's purpose and those certain marks which define it.

The Ezzos and Bucknams each had certain values they wanted to instill within their children to help them understand that they were part of something bigger than themselves. This is how family identity is formed. It's not something that simply happens—it will only come through conscious effort and by design.

We would often tell our children how glad we were to be part of such a great family. We had regular family nights together. We took vacations together, allowing the children to plan whole segments of the trip. We had talk times. We shared our values, helping them form their own moral system.

You want your house to feel like home base, a place where every member of your family feels like the other members are the "home team crowd" rooting him on. Remember the discussion of the interdependent family, in which all members are facing inward for support, counsel, and camaraderie? This is what you're shooting for in your family.

Family identity is critically important as a child enters the teen years. We have always believed that children who receive comfort and approval from a close-knit family tend to look to those relationships for support as they move through adolescence. Within the comfortable confines of such a family, it is parents, not peers, who usually have the greater influence.

Teens choose their friends according to whether their family identity is accepted or rejected. If a teen chooses his family as the primary source of values and comfort, his friends will be kids with like values. When there is harmony between the core beliefs of parents and children, children will gravitate to families and friends with similar values. This creates positive peer pressure.

On the other hand, a teen who has been unable to rely upon his family to be his source of support and affection will be dependent on outside influences to meet these basic social needs. He is more likely to be sensitive to group pressures and disapproval. The tendency for these children is to move in the direction of peers and to become indifferent toward nonpeer influences, such as parents.

Negative peer pressure on a teen is only as strong as family identity is weak. When the family identity is strengthened, the voice of peer pressure begins to fade. *You* want to be the source of your child's acceptance, affection, and values.

Now, how do you achieve it? Even in the closest of human relationships, that of a parent and child, there is no guarantee of future rapport. Though both parties contribute to the strong or poor outcomes in the relationship, for the most part, parents remain in the driver's seat. They greatly influence the outcome by the choices they make.

Cultivate a Positive Family Identity

If you want to build a trusting relationship with your children, start by cultivating attitudes that lead to a strong sense of family identity. Family identity is based on trust, acceptance, and a growing loyalty between members. It is a significant factor in the life of every child.

In the Ezzo and Bucknam households, family ties were never optional. We didn't wake up one day and ask our children if they wanted to belong to our family. From the beginning we instilled into them that we had been put together into the family to love, encourage, and support one another.

Each member of the family knew the team was counting on every other member to stay committed to the code of ethics held by the family. Consistent loyalty to our family values sealed our identity as a unit. Even today, whether together or apart, both families are committed to those mutual standards.

One way to enhance family identity is to verbalize your commitment to your family whenever appropriate. Tell them how much you love them individually and as a unit. This is especially critical for fathers. Dad cannot be a mere spectator, observing Mom's efforts to hold the family together. Dad must be an active leader and participant in the process. While driving or sitting around the dinner table, encourage your family by making statements such as, "This is really a terrific family. I am so thankful we're together," or "You kids have the best mom in the world," or "I'd rather be here with you guys than anywhere else, with anyone else, doing anything else!"

Why is such verbalization important? When parents, especially fathers, are excited about the family, children feel the same way. But when Dad is silent about the family, the question lingers in their minds—"Does he really care about us?"

Parents sometimes think that by not talking, they are not communicating anything to their kids. Not so. With your silence you communicate disinterest, or worse, parental disapproval or rejection. As your child sees and hears that Dad and Mom are on board with the family, his confidence in you grows.

BE VULNERABLE TO YOUR TEEN

With a family identity worth investing in in place, you can start employing strategies to attract investors. One such strategy is to give your teenager freedom to point out and help you with your blind spots.

You're probably saying, "Are you serious?" Being vulnerable before your teenagers can be as difficult as asking for their forgiveness. It may seem risky or frightening, but it has been proven to be an effective way to help get healthy parent/teen relations back on track. Since your teen has lived with you for thirteen to nineteen years, he or she is all too aware of your weaknesses. Being imperfect is easy for parents. Accepting responsibility for imperfections is hard.

One characteristic of strong families is the freedom each member feels to lovingly confront one another when necessary. Sensitivity and wisdom must be applied for such interaction to be effective. Both parties must be open to learning. And the individual being confronted must be willing to listen. The purpose of this confrontation is not to condemn but to strengthen; it is not to incite conflict but to rouse one another to love and good works.

The Ezzos practiced this principle in their own family. As parents, they knew they had parenting blind spots—wrong perspectives, lack of patience, occasional overconfidence in their decisions or too little confidence in their children's. They knew their teens saw all their frailties. Realizing that no one wanted them to know the truth more than their own children did, they invited, even encouraged, the girls to help their parents become better human beings. In doing so, they communicated to their children that their parents trusted their motives and discernment. That spoke volumes to their daughters.

First, they set up some guidelines governing this privilege.

1. Teens cannot verbally assault their parents. They must speak honestly and honorably at all times.
2. Both teens and parents must be in agreement on the particular weakness or weaknesses to be worked on.
3. Teens must come with a desire to help, not simply to accuse.
4. Teens must be in control of their own attitudes when making an observation or accusation.
5. Struggling teens must want to start over. Their willingness to do so validates their desire to have a relationship with Mom and Dad.

Although these rules are designed for teens confronting their parents, the same principles should be used when parents confront their teens.

There are some advantages to giving your teens the freedom to work on your weaknesses. First, it fosters within you a healthy vulnerability. One of the keys to unlocking the door to the human heart is a humble spirit. To be vulnerable is to be open to the censure or criticism of morally mature members of the family. Teens detest hypocrisy in their parents; parents' vulnerability and openness to their input helps prevent it.

A second advantage is that when you do this, your teen makes an investment in the parent/teen relationship. If you have trusted

COURTING FAMILY INVESTORS

him to tell you about yourself, you've left yourself open for harm. Sometimes a teen will abuse this privilege and kick you when your defenses are down. That's the chance you take anytime you are truly honest with someone. Try not to get offended or strike back. If you and your teen have been at odds for a while, it will take some time for both sides to lay down their weapons. Your consistency will be the key. Keep at it. Stay vulnerable. Keep the goal in mind.

Your teen wants to invest in you and in the family. But first you must give her a healthy prospect of real rewards for her investment—yourself.

SHARE A MEAL TOGETHER EVERY DAY

Families need to be together in order to flourish. The destination of the independent family, in which every member fends for himself, is not familial bliss. But a family that intentionally spends time in each other's presence—without the TV on or friends over—is a family working toward becoming interdependent.

But we're all so busy. Especially when a teenager gets that driver's license, it can be almost impossible to get everyone together at once. Because time demands can loosen family ties and put serious strain on already weak ones, extra effort must be put into keeping the family together. Time to cast another mooring line to the pier.

That's why the Ezzos committed themselves to regrouping each night at mealtime. That sometimes meant their schedules had to change. But they were committed to having one meal together each day—to relax, to talk, to recharge their emotional batteries, to find out what was going on in each other's lives, and to enjoy the growing friendship with their teenagers.

127

Your family's schedules may be so spread out that hoping to share a meal a day would belong in the realm of science fiction. If this is so, start small. Aim for one meal a month. Then shoot for once every two weeks. Then once a week. You'd be surprised how much good can come from one meal taken together every week. Your next goal might be three meals a week. The point is to be together as a family, so the more meals you can share the better.

ALLOW YOUR TEEN TO PLAN A FAMILY NIGHT

Some people think having leisure-time activities with their children is a luxury. It is not. It is an absolute necessity. Family night helps keep your work and play in perspective.

The Ezzos planned a family night once a week. It was a time when they separated themselves from work and school and came together for family fun. Family night afforded them an informal setting for relaxing with family members who didn't care how anyone's hair looked or what anyone wore.

They eventually added a little twist to their weekly family fun night. Long before their children reached the teen years, they took ownership for every other family night. They did a little budget and planned the evening. The family played board and card games, had indoor picnics, or feasted on pizza and fondue and watched a favorite video classic.

What are the benefits of a family night? Your children are not just taking ownership of a family night every other week, they are actually taking ownership of your family. It is their investment into the fun portion of other family members' lives. This also ensures that your children don't end up with your leftover time.

Plan a weekly family night. It adds another good reason for your teenagers to stick around.

ALLOW YOUR TEEN TO PLAN A VACATION

If letting them plan a family night causes teens to buy into the family, imagine what would happen if they could plan a whole trip!

Whether it's going to be a weekend camping trip or a two-weeklong event, if your teen is involved in planning it, you can be sure you'll have buy-in. Of course, we need to be realistic here. Spur of the moment jaunts to Paris may be the trip of choice for your teen but not exactly feasible (unless it's Paris, Texas). Gently lay some ground rules, remembering that the more good memories you have together, the closer you will grow as an interdependent family.

For years, some friends of the Ezzos left the February cold of northern New England to spend two weeks in warm Florida. Each year they returned home discouraged by their children's constant complaints and lack of appreciation for all that the parents had done.

Then one year someone suggested they let their kids help plan the next family trip. That included letting them help decide the travel route, make some of the scheduling decisions, and select some of the special events they would attend along the way.

It made all the difference in the world. The children became participants in the vacation instead of merely spectators. And the overall benefit? The work that went into planning and scheduling, the anticipation of seeing those plans realized, and their sense of ownership all factored into building lasting memories for each member of that family.

We really hope you'll try this. Just imagine the most rebellious teen loving every minute of a family vacation. This could be the moment when things begin to change.

TAKE WALKS TOGETHER

Why not take a stroll with your teen? It could be around the block or down the beach or over to the park. You never know what conversations might come up. Take a walk today.

If your response to this is, "Yeah, right—three hundred years ago maybe," give it a chance. It may surprise you that this simple suggestion might get accepted. The Ezzos found that taking walks with their daughters, one at a time, often led to very personal and private conversations with their girls. There is something about a twenty-minute walk that causes people to reflect, open up, and share their hearts.

Walking with your teen will give her access to you and give you access to her. She may expose her inner thoughts, fears, doubts, and hopes. Sometimes she may just need to talk, which will make those walks good times for you to just listen. Not everything you will hear will always make sense, but that's all right. Your listening will serve a purpose: It will provide a sounding board to help your teenager sort things out. After a talk like that, you may hear a heartfelt, "Thanks for listening, Mom and Dad." Talk about your parenting rewards!

EMPATHIZE

Gary knew something was wrong one day when he saw his daughter Jenny come home from high school. Her eyes were downcast and her shoulders drooped.

"Jen, you look like you're hurting," Gary said. "It's obvious that it hasn't been a good day. I'm sorry about that."

She looked at her dad with a halfhearted smile, "It's nothing, Dad."

Gary decided not to pry. He remembered more than one occasion when a person's "Do you want to talk about it?" put him off. Sometimes we need to pick with whom and when we share troubles. His statement let her know that he cared.

Later that afternoon, Gary was weeding his garden when Jenny came outside, pulled up a crate, and sat down. She started talking about Martha, a new girl she had befriended. It seemed that Martha had also become friends with Jenny's best friend, Sarah. Suddenly, Jenny was no longer included in Martha and Sarah's plans. She had been nudged out and made to feel like a fifth wheel.

Jennifer asked, "Why, Dad, after all these years of being best friends, would Sarah just drop me like that? Sarah wears Martha's clothes and her jewelry and goes home with her after school. And she has only known her for a couple of weeks."

"It hurts when that happens," Gary said. "How could it not hurt to watch your best friend take off with the new kid, especially one you introduced her to?"

Jenny reacted curiously to that statement. It never occurred to her that one of her parents might have lost a best friend in a similar manner. Gary began to tell her about a similar incident from his own youth.

Afterward Jenny asked, "What do you think I should do?"

Bingo: a heart-to-heart. Gary and his daughter shared a moment of trust and heartfelt connection. It's a memory they will both cherish.

For a teen struggling with life, there is no more important

resource than a parent who can empathize. Letting our kids know that we understand what they are feeling because we have been there ourselves serves to tighten the relational ties. It is a concrete way for them to know we truly do understand.

A week later, Jennifer came waltzing into Gary's office after school. She wore a smile that lit up the room. "Dad, Sarah wrote me a note today and apologized for being such a jerk. She told me how wrong she had been to think that all of Martha's beautiful clothes and flashy jewelry could ever replace me. She wants us to be best friends like we always have been."

After a warm hug, Jenny whispered, "Thanks, Dad."

Empathy breeds confidence in parental counsel. Offer yourself to your kids. Share your failures and your successes, your hurts and pains. Tell them the stories of your childhood struggles. We all had them. When your teen awakens to the fact that every generation experiences similar relational testing and trials, he will turn to you with confidence.

SUMMARY

Today life seems to be speeding by faster than ever before. It feels as if the pace of everything has been accelerated, including the rate at which our children grow. Within a few years, your teenager will enter adulthood. When that happens, will he have fond memories of family interactions? Will he be anchored to you because of them?

We believe that children naturally desire to be close to their parents. You are your child's first models for life and love and relationships. So much of how well your child does as an adult depends almost solely on the relationship she has with you.

As you move through this day and week and month, look for ways to build connections between you and your teen. We're sure you can come up with many more creative ways to do this with your family. When you've got the goal clearly in mind—trying to attract family members to the family itself—and when you've got a commitment to make it happen, you'll find new ideas popping up all the time.

Are you prepared to be delighted at the new friendships that are about to bud?

BRINGING IT HOME

1. What is family identity, and why is it important?
2. What are some of the distinctive marks of your family's identity?
3. What are the main advantages of asking your teenager to help you in your areas of weakness?
4. What is the benefit of allowing your teen to help plan a family night or vacation?
5. Why should you empathize with your teen?

Chapter Eight

Love Languages

Several years ago, Gary visited Russia at the dawn of their new republic. On one of his free afternoons he visited historical Red Square just outside the Kremlin. As he began to take in the incredible splendor, he noticed a crowd gathering in front of one of its monuments. The monument turned out to be Lenin's tomb. The crowd had gathered to watch the famous changing of the guards. Gary found himself surrounded by a crowd of Russian-speaking spectators. Since Gary doesn't speak Russian, the sound was all a blare.

As the replacement guards began to march to the tomb, the spectators began taking pictures, pointing at the scene unfolding before them. Suddenly, to Gary's left, he heard a familiar sound.

"Hey, Larry! Come over here. You can get a great picture."

Instantly, Gary tuned in. Why? Because someone was speaking his native language. No one else turned toward the other two Americans. For one obvious reason: They didn't speak English. And while they quickly realized another language was being spoken, they could not relate to it.

While the crowd at the tomb stretched to see the event, Gary accidentally bumped into the man standing behind him. Gary turned his head and said "Excuse me." Although those words came to him spontaneously, he realized the person he spoke to had no idea what he just said. While English was Gary's primary language and the one he would naturally speak, it did not make sense to his neighbor.

The events of that afternoon provide a great analogy for the love language phenomena because what happens with spoken languages also occurs with emotional languages. We all tend to speak our primary emotional language, but it often comes across to other people as an unknown tongue. We say "I love you" in one language, while they say it in another. As a result, our efforts to demonstrate love can be frustrated or misunderstood. We have to learn to truly communicate in the language of the people we love.

DOES ANYONE HERE SPEAK FLEMISH?

To achieve that goal, we must learn what the basic love languages are and learn the primary love languages of each of our family members. The good news is that you can master love languages, unlike Russian, by the time you finish reading this chapter.

The love languages concept was developed in 1972 by Judson Swihart in his book, *How to Say I Love You* (Downer's Grove, Ill.: Intervarsity Press, 1972). It was popularized in the nineties by Dr. Gary Chapman in his books, *The Five Love Languages: How to Express Heartfelt Commitment to Your Mate*, *The Five Love Languages of Children*, and others. Don't miss Dr. Chapman's book on love languages for teenagers: *The Five Love Languages of Teenagers*. We heartily recommend these books for a fuller treatment of love languages.

Scenario One

Bill and Sally had a good marriage, yet the full sensation of love was missing. They knew they loved each other but also felt frustrated in communicating it. It turned out that Bill's primary love language was physical touch and closeness. He spoke that language and felt loved when it was spoken to him. The language that meant the least to him was words of encouragement, which happened to be Sally's primary language. Last on her list was physical touch and closeness.

This couple loved each other but didn't know how to communicate their love in a common language. Bill often would ask his wife, "How about a hug?" In turn, Sally wished that Bill would write her more notes and letters, like he did when they were dating. She wanted to hear words of encouragement, while he desired physical touch and closeness. Sally would do many special things in the front yard, hoping that when Bill walked through the door he would say, "The rose garden looks beautiful. Thank you for your efforts." Bill did notice the garden and appreciate her work, but rarely would he communicate his pleasure with words of encouragement. And he felt isolated because she didn't give him the physical contact he craved.

At a seminar addressing the five love languages, Bill and Sally learned what was going on. It was a real eye-opener for them, and it revolutionized their marriage. Bill now says "I love you" with words of encouragement, both verbally and with notes left around the house. Sally now initiates hand-holding and hugs, and she stands close to Bill at social gatherings. As a result of learning to speak in each other's primary language, the fullness of love has returned to their marriage.

Scenario Two

For twenty-five years, Betty begrudgingly accepted the many gifts her husband, Mike, bought for her. Time and time again she'd think, *This is frivolous. I don't need this.* Occasionally, she would catch a glimpse of hurt in Mike's face but would dismiss it. After all, it was just a gift.

Later, Betty learned about the five love languages and instantly recognized what her husband had been doing. When she realized that she'd been rejecting her husband's expressions of love to her, she wept. What compounded her sorrow was learning that gift giving was on the bottom of her list of love languages and that she rarely spoke that language to him—except at holidays.

How discouraging it is to say, "I love you," only to be rejected time and time again! Betty learned the hard way that we must not only learn to speak the primary love language of our partner but also learn to receive graciously all the expressions of love that come our way from those around us.

LOVE LANGUAGE SURVEY

What does love look like to you? Does it mean just being there to listen? Does it mean doing some quiet act of service to help someone succeed? Does it mean picking up a little gift that just says you were thinking about someone when you were apart? Does it mean making sure someone knows how much you appreciate what he's done? Does it mean cuddling up next to that special someone and just being close?

Children have primary and secondary love languages just as adults do. Discovering your teen's love language may be a huge revelation to you. Coming to understand how family members express and accept love has saved many marriages and families and has strengthened countless others. Our hope is that it will do the same for yours.

We've provided a survey to help you determine what your primary love language is. Many find they have more than one—some even say they have all five! We all like self-discovery, so let's get going! Below are five groupings of five statements, one statement for each love language. Read the sentences, then score them on a 5–1 scale, with 5 being the statement that *most* makes you feel loved.

If you feel you already know your love language, it would be easy to just look for that one and mark it with a 5 every time. But we encourage you to really read all five statements in each grouping. You might be surprised at what you find if you really evaluate yourself. Plus, it will help you find your secondary languages. And it's just as important to know how you *don't* express love as how you do.

When you've finished the test for yourself, do it again and again, once for each member of your family.

Which statement makes you feel most loved (5 = most; 1 = least)?

Group One

> A ___ Your spouse/teenager/parent says: "You really did a great job on that. I appreciate it."
>
> B ___ Your spouse/teenager/parent unexpectedly does something in or around the house or your room that you appreciate.
>
> C ___ Your spouse/teenager/parent brings you home a surprise treat from the store.

D ___ Your spouse/teenager/parent invites you to go on a leisurely walk just to chat.

E ___ Your spouse/teenager/parent makes a point to embrace and kiss you before leaving the house.

Group Two

A ___ Your spouse/teenager/parent tells you how much he or she appreciates you.

B ___ Your spouse/teenager/parent (male) volunteers to do the dishes and encourages you to relax. Your spouse/teenager/parent (female) volunteers to wash your car and encourages you to relax.

C ___ Your spouse/teenager/parent (male) brings you flowers, just because he cares. Your spouse/teenager/parent (female) brings you home a special food treat from the local bakery.

D ___ Your spouse/teenager/parent invites you to sit down and talk about your day.

E ___ Your spouse/teenager/parent enjoys receiving a hug even when you're just passing by room to room.

Group Three

A ___ Your spouse/teenager/parent tells everyone at a party about a recent success you had.

B ___ Your spouse/teenager/parent cleans out your car.

C ___ Your spouse/teenager/parent surprises you with an unexpected gift.

D ___ Your spouse/teenager/parent surprises you with a special afternoon trip.

E ___ Your spouse holds your hand as you walk through the mall, or your teenager/parent stands by your side with an arm around your shoulder at a public event.

Group Four

A ___ Your spouse/teenager/parent praises you about one of your special qualities.

B ___ Your spouse/teenager/parent brings you breakfast in bed.

C ___ Your spouse/teenager/parent surprises you with a membership to something you always wanted.

D ___ Your spouse/teenager/parent plans a special night out for the two of you.

E ___ Your spouse/teenager/parent will personally drive you to an event instead of you having to go on the old crowded bus with the team.

Group Five

A ___ Your spouse/teenager/parent tells you how much his or her friends appreciate you.

B ___ Your spouse/teenager/parent takes the time to fill out the long, complicated applications that you had hoped to get to this evening.

C ___ Your spouse/teenager/parent sends you something special through the mail.

D ___ Your spouse/teenager/parent kidnaps you for lunch and takes you to your favorite restaurant.

E ___ Your spouse/teenager/parent gives you a massage.

Score Sheet

Transfer your scores from your test questions to this scoring profile.

	Encouraging Words	Acts of Service	Gift Giving	Quality Time	Physical Touch
Group 1	A___	B___	C___	D___	E___
Group 2	A___	B___	C___	D___	E___
Group 3	A___	B___	C___	D___	E___
Group 4	A___	B___	C___	D___	E___
Group 5	A___	B___	C___	D___	E___
Totals	A___	B___	C___	D___	E___

This test measures how you primarily desire to receive love, but that will also tell you how you probably find yourself expressing love. You'll have to work backwards a bit with other people you take the test for. For each grouping, mark down which of the five ways your family member usually expresses love. From that you can determine how she needs to have love expressed back to her.

When you're done, write down from the primary to the least of the love languages of each family member in the blanks below. Compare your primary language with that of your other family members.

1._____

2._____

3._____

4._____

5._____

Does that explain a few things?

Now that your curiosity is piqued, here's more on each of the love languages. This will help you refine your answers and maybe help you decide between two or more that seem to be neck and neck for the primary language for you or someone you desire to show love to.

LOVE LANGUAGE NUMBER ONE: WORDS OF AFFIRMATION AND ENCOURAGEMENT

One way of expressing love is verbally, through words of encouragement. In healthy relationships, verbal affirmation is never redundant. Each of us enjoys receiving a pat on the back or hearing "well done" from someone we respect. We appreciate hearing how our actions pleased someone or that somebody has simply taken notice of our efforts.

"That dress really shows off your blue eyes."

"I was very proud of the way you handled that situation with your brother."

"You look so handsome."

"One thing I can always count on from you is a willingness to help."

We all love words of encouragement, but someone whose primary love language is words of encouragement survives on them. Your teens are no different. They are encouraged when justified praise comes their way. If we are not verbalizing our encouragement, what message are we sending?

Verbally encourage your teen in the little things and the big even if you don't think it's his primary love language. It might be an important secondary one. Besides, it's a healthy habit for you to adopt when speaking to anyone, especially your own children. Sometimes a simple "Thank you" can go a long way.

If you are just getting started on the encouragement side of your relationship, be careful not to flatter or to qualify your encouragement. Flattery is insincere, by definition, and teens hate insincerity. And a mixed encouragement, something like "You look lovely in that dress now that you've almost got all that flab off," isn't going to fill your teen's love language tank one drop.

Verbally affirming someone is a powerful way of saying "I love you." For some, very possibly for your teen, it is the main way they "hear" love and know they're truly valued.

Keep an ear out for praise and encouragement coming to you from others. If this isn't your primary language, you may brush the comments aside as trivial. But the other person is very likely tipping her hand about how she speaks love. Take note.

LOVE LANGUAGE NUMBER TWO: ACTS OF SERVICE

Another way to say "I love you" is through acts of service. This means doing something special for another person, something you know he or she will appreciate. Normally, this is something outside the realm of everyday routine.

Gail Bucknam drives her kids to school Monday through Friday. Ten round trips require at least one stop at the gas station every week. Gail is very capable of tending to the need, but she greatly appreciates it when her husband, Bob, fills the van on Sunday night so she won't have to worry about it.

Typically in any household with one or more teens, things get fairly hectic. This was true years ago in the Ezzo household, and

LOVE LANGUAGES

sometimes their children's rooms showed it. Although their children were normally good at keeping their rooms neat, there were seasons of clutter, especially during exam times. On occasion, Anne Marie Ezzo would clean their rooms for them. She realized how busy the girls were and wanted to communicate her love, appreciation, and thanks in a tangible way. She did something that she knew her children would appreciate over and above all that a mother normally would do during these years.

Again, watch for signs of acts of service speakers around you. If your teen goes above and beyond what she needs to do as a member of the family, taking care of details and chores for you, leaving you free to do other work, she deserves notice. She's expressing love in a beautiful way. Now, if your love language is words of affirmation, you might sit her down and thank her profusely for what she's done. But wouldn't it be even better if you thanked her by doing some small service for her?

LOVE LANGUAGE NUMBER THREE: GIFT GIVING

Kevin's mother and father noticed that on each trip to the store, he consistently asked for money to buy something. For years, they interpreted his requests as an abnormal materialistic hang-up. They worked to break him of that trait but had no success.

When Kevin's parents learned about love languages, they realized that their son's primary love language was gift giving. Now they understood the mysterious obsession with little purchases. When they went to the store now, they made sure to bring him little gifts: a pack of gum, some pencils, a twenty-ounce bottle of his favorite soft drink. Nothing expensive, just a little something to say

"I love you." That practice virtually eliminated his requests for things in the store.

Even no-cost gestures can pack great meaning for someone with this language because of what they represent. Impromptu gift giving sends the message, "When we are apart, you are on my mind. This gift is a token reflecting my thoughts of you." The deed goes even deeper into the heart when the gift is the other person's favorite color or is something they collect. This type of gift adds this message: "I'm paying attention to you and noting what you care about."

Gift giving is the primary love language of the Ezzos' youngest daughter, Jennifer. Many times her parents entered their home to hear Jenny say, "I made you a surprise." Whether she baked a cake, pie, or cookies, she was saying "I love you" through gift giving. In this case, she didn't give something she had purchased but a gift she had made as an act of love.

Realizing Jenny's primary love language helped Gary and Anne Marie direct their expressions of love. Sometimes showing love for her meant bringing home a pretty ribbon for her hair or something as simple as a tube of Chapstick. It was not the gift that caused the sense of being loved to swell in Jennifer's heart, but the love behind the act.

Are you receiving silly gifts from family members? Do they come back from the store and hand you a discount CD they bought you, one that is sort of along the lines of music you like? Do they buy you a flavor of ice cream you enjoy even though the freezer's full of sweets already? Watch out! They may be telling you how much they love you. But if you don't recognize it as that, you could be stomping on something fragile.

LOVE LANGUAGE NUMBER FOUR: QUALITY TIME

Fourteen-year-old Cindy answered her mom's routine questions about her day with one-word answers. Mom thought her increasingly defiant daughter just wasn't interested in talking. So, in an earnest desire to demonstrate her love, she promised Cindy a big birthday party and took Cindy out shopping for a complete wardrobe of all the latest. Still, she yearned to learn what was happening in her child's heart. Yet every time she pressed, Cindy would just blow up.

To Mom's dismay, Cindy began seeking counsel and support from other moms in her social group. She even called them on the phone and requested time alone together to "just talk." Cindy's mom was frustrated. Why could the girl talk to other mothers but not to her?

She failed to see what Cindy so desperately needed: quality time spent in heart-to-heart communication with her own dear mother. Her mom was saying "I love you" with gifts, but Cindy's primary love language was quality time. Instead of trips to the mall and ornate party invitations, Cindy just wanted a walk in the park or a quiet lunch out alone with Mom.

Quality time is not sitting on the couch reading the newspaper or watching television together. That might satisfy someone whose love language is physical closeness, but it will only frustrate someone who needs love in the form of quality time.

Quality time means that you focus on the person talking to you, not glancing half the time at the TV. It means you truly listen to what she's saying. If you are distracted by something else, you send the message that not only what this person is saying but that *this person* is not important to you. Half listening is a discourtesy to anyone, but if you do it to a quality timer, you can cause great injury.

Quality timers like to just sit and talk. They tend to talk about serious matters and are often willing to divulge heartfelt fears or aspirations. It's the time spent learning about the other person's thoughts and feelings that matters to someone who speaks and hears love in this way. The time you spend together may only be ten minutes, but for the person whose love language is quality time, those ten minutes are precious.

Do people around you seem to demand your time? And when you finally grant them some, is what they have to say not very important? Maybe they just want to tell you what happened at school or even just hear about your day. Take heed! This person may be speaking to you in the language of quality time. You may not think that what he has to say is anything of great consequence, but if you take the time to really listen and interact with him, you'll make him feel as if he is of great consequence to you.

LOVE LANGUAGE NUMBER FIVE: PHYSICAL CLOSENESS/TOUCH

The language of physical touch (or physical closeness) is another way of saying "I love you." Holding hands, putting your arm around your spouse's or child's shoulder, warm hugs, or just standing close to each other can telegraph a special love message.

Here's an example. A husband is working in the garden, and his wife sits down nearby with a book and begins to read. She could have read the book anywhere in the house, but she chose to be close to her husband.

This transmits love, especially to someone who speaks this language. Some couples enjoy being near each other even when silence prevails. Simply knowing the other person is nearby can confirm a partner's affection and care. Here's where just watching TV together can fill up someone's love tank.

To hold and be held communicates vulnerability and a closeness that is reserved for trusting members of a family. For some parents this may mean simply placing a hand on their son or daughter's shoulder and saying, "Great game," or "Great job," or "Thank you." Other times it may be a high-five or a hug. Our point is this: Don't underestimate the influence of physical encouragement. For some teens there is no greater way of hearing "I love you" than through touch.

Is someone in your family always grabbing and touching and climbing into your lap? Does she follow you from room to room? When you say you want to be alone, does it hurt her more than you think it should? You may have a physical closeness speaker in your house.

It doesn't take much to make this person feel loved: Just be with her. If you're going to read a book, do it where she can be near you. If you're going to sit on the couch, sit close to her. If you're sitting together at a movie theater, put your arm around her. These people need time with you, but it doesn't even have to be focused time (as with a quality timer). You can peel onions together or run errands together or take out the trash together. The point isn't what you do, but that you do it *with* your physical closeness loved one.

SUMMARY

Even if you never learn to speak Russian, you can certainly learn to speak in other love languages. You may not like sitting on the couch with your teen if you're not really *doing* anything. But if your teen's love language is physical closeness, you are communicating your love to him.

You may find your family members experimenting in how to express love to you, too. If your love language is gift giving, someone may shyly hand you a pack of gum picked up at the grocery store. Make sure you praise the effort. Better yet, make sure you reward the effort in the giver's own love language.

You may not understand why a simple act of service you do for someone means anything to someone else. But when it does work, when it lights up your loved one's face and enhances your relationship across the board, we guarantee you'll do it again.

So open up your love lexicon and start picking up a new language.

BRINGING IT HOME

Have each of your teens work through the love language test for themselves. Compare your findings and talk about how you can better express and receive love now that you know each other's love languages.

Chapter Nine

Dating, Courtship, and Readiness for Marriage

One of the most important aspects of the teen years is the discovery of the opposite sex. Suddenly your teenager is interested in style, fashion, makeup, acne control, and going to the right places at the right times to see the right people. Schools start having dances and banquets and homecoming games. And boys start calling on your daughter—or your boy starts calling on other people's daughters.

It can be a terrifying time for parents. You may wonder how in the world you're going to get your teen through these years without irreparable damage, especially with regard to sex. Will your teen be sexually active? You have to know there will be pressure to be so. Will your daughter get pregnant? Will she ask to go on birth control pills? Will she have an abortion or be a mother by the time she's fifteen? Will your son cause one or more of these problems?

You may have in your mind an image of your grown child married to a wonderful spouse, living an ideal life. But between you and that goal lie the teenage years. The path seems to be writhing with grasping vines and beset with hidden pits. And there seems to be no time to figure out how to set out across this expanse, because even now your teen wants a ride to the mall where you suspect there's going to be a rendezvous.

IT'S A DATE

Fifty years ago, a typical date was going for pizza and a movie. Sometimes a date today can be going straight to a hotel for more than pizza.

Frightening, isn't it?

We have been delighted to witness the abstinence movement that has swept America. It's not an antidating movement, just an antipremarital sex movement. Teenagers across the nation are choosing to remain sexually pure, preserving themselves for their future marriage partners. We are especially pleased to see this trend because so many of these teens are choosing abstinence without their parents' intervention.

We won't say that dating itself is wrong. Both of us authors dated several girls before marrying our wives. But we will say that sometimes the contemporary context of dating creates conditions that could be hurtful to young people. What makes dating acceptable or unacceptable is the age of participants, the appropriateness of the relationship, the context of dating, and the motive for dating.

The question isn't whether or not dating is bad, but whether it creates a false expectation of commitment that can never be fulfilled. We think it can, especially when it gets into the boyfriend/girlfriend stage. Teenagers are expected to commit to a monogamous relationship that is designed to be temporary. How can this reinforce the idea that marriage is designed to be a *permanent* monogamous relationship?

Young people are giving away their hearts too early, then having them broken. They're getting their emotions stirred, then having them trampled. When you consider the pressure from peer groups for teen couples to get involved sexually, the whole idea of dating seems less advisable than ever.

It used to be that the common moral community acted as a de facto chaperon. There was social and peer pressure to act properly on a date. Today peer pressure doesn't keep teenagers away from sex, it pushes them toward it. The climate can be such that, especially for girls, if the young man buys his date a nice dinner, she may feel she is sexually obligated to him.

One popular alternative to one-on-one dating is group dating. The Ezzo girls went out every Friday night with four or five kids. The members of the group were from homes within our moral community, so we knew the teens would share a moral standard we approved of. They had as much fun and probably more fun than if they'd gone out with just one person. One reason this was attractive to them was that they realized, as young people are realizing today, that at age seventeen or eighteen or nineteen, they weren't wanting to get married. Why establish a long-term relationship with someone if neither party is ready for marriage?

Perhaps when you were younger, you did not abstain, yet now you wish to urge your teenager not to repeat your mistake. This might be a great opportunity to be vulnerable with your teen and give part of your story. You don't need to go into all the details of your past, but if you realize now that you really wish you had abstained and you give good reasons for abstinence, your teen may be willing to listen. Nothing beats a personal testimonial.

DATING VS. COURTSHIP

Dating, as the word is used today, implies a casual, recreational relationship between two people who usually have no intention of marrying each other anytime soon. It can be a very useful and fun way of extending friendships and exploring compatibility. It's a way for young people to find out the kinds of things they like and don't like in members of the opposite sex, helping them refine what they're looking for in a future spouse.

As we said above, we have nothing against the idea of dating, per se. What we object to is the environment of dating in which teens are urged to engage in sexual activity. We can applaud parents who decide to restrict their teenagers' dating, and we can applaud parents who allow their teens to date (though we hope they lay out some clear parameters for their teens).

At the same time, we do think group dating is a great alternative. It retains the benefits of dating, having fun and exploring compatibility, and the group of like-minded teens acts as a source of positive peer pressure, reinforcing moral behavior for all its members.

There are special occasions in which datelike arrangements might be appropriate. One of the Ezzo daughters elected to go to her ninth grade banquet. She dined in the beautifully decorated school gymnasium with the rest of her class. The young man who accompanied her was not her *date* so much as her *escort* for the evening. It was a fun event, but a one time occurrence. There was no commitment on either side for beyond that evening. For everything else, we recommend either group dating or courtship.

Courtship refers to a type of activity whose goal is marriage. It is the attempt on the part of a young man to win the affections of a young woman's heart, with the express purpose of entering into matrimony. Courtship was the primary method of wooing in previous centuries until it was replaced by dating sometime after World War II. There's no reason courtship can't be revived, and in fact, we are seeing a resurgence of the practice already.

We fully realize that courtship is not for everybody. What we describe may strike you as highly ideal. If your daughter has just had her boyfriend's name, Snake, tattooed on her chin, the thought that they might enter formal courtship might give you a good laugh. But read this section anyway. You may find that you like what you see and decide to adapt it to your situation, if not in Snake's case, then maybe for your younger children.

Apples and Oranges: Dating and Courtship Compared

Courting and dating are not synonymous. Here are some important differences to note.

First, courtship requires age-readiness for marriage. Dating, on the other hand, usually allows younger teens premature access to the type of committed, male/female relationship that should be reserved for courtship and marriage. This can be very damaging emotionally. The frequent comings and goings of boyfriend/girlfriend relationships do not engender stability, but self-doubt and fragility. Because many teens do not yet have the skills to keep their emotions in check, dating can open the door for all kinds of exploitation, from being taken advantage of financially and socially to surrendering oneself sexually.

Second, courtship presupposes the possibility of a mature love relationship that will lead to engagement. Dating makes no such assumption. Most kids date because they're looking for a good time in the here and now. They have come to expect a level of entertainment from a dating partner. But if the fun runs dry, teens don't drop dating, they drop their date. They look for someone new to please them. We believe this builds wrong expectations for marriage. Because courtship is not so transitory, it is a better preparation for marriage.

Third, courtship considers factors beyond just the couple, such as parents, family and extended family, belief systems, values, and personal convictions. Consideration is given to how a couple's decisions might affect other important relationships. Not so with dating, which is confined to a single, narrow activity—the date itself. What takes place between the pickup and drop-off is the only thing that really matters to the dating couple.

Fourth, courtship is a means to an end: engagement. Dating is an end unto itself. The emphasis in dating is usually present and momentary satisfaction, not the possibility of choosing a spouse or preparing for marriage.

Courtship, then, is the prelude to a possible engagement. Its purpose is to provide a couple with time to discover, assess, and evaluate their compatibility as potential lifelong marriage partners. Courtship isn't a time of experimentation but of exploration.

Courtship is not a guarantee of engagement but a measured step toward it. Both the couple involved in the relationship and their parents have the freedom to pull the reins if things are not going as they should. The closer two people grow together, the more the underlying (and not necessarily pleasant) habits begin to show themselves. That's why neither teens nor parents should rush toward courtship without some mechanism for stopping the process.

THE THREE PHASES OF COURTSHIP

Courtship naturally unfolds in three phases: exploration, confirmation, and pledging. Each phase brings a new level of responsibility and unique challenges to the couple, and each phase allows for either person to pull in the reins and slow down the process.

There is no set time limit for these phases. Couples will pass through each phase on a timetable unique to their relational needs and expectations. There are a variety of factors that will influence the length of each phase, including the maturity of the couple, parental favor, and the comfort level of the couple themselves.

Phase One: Exploration

Courtship is not for young teens. It is for older teens (or twenty-somethings or beyond) who are of an age and a maturity level at which they can rightly consider marriage. Nor is courtship for strangers. Your son or daughter should only enter into a courtship relationship with someone who is already a good friend. Best friends make the best spouses. If a young man and woman know they get along well, it's natural for them to take the next step. Entering into courtship is acknowledging that marriage is a possibility but not a promise.

The first phase of courtship is an exploratory phase. Its purpose is to allow the couple to discover and explore their emotions for each other beyond the level of simple friendship. Their commitments are forming and being tried out. Each learns to rearrange his or her life for the benefit of the other. Each begins to understand the give-and-take necessary to meet the other person's needs while still getting his or her own needs met. They enjoy the pleasant aspects of each other's personalities, discovering wonderful things they never knew. They also discover not-so-wonderful things they never knew. They find out whether they can live with those things or if it's just too much.

Phase Two: Confirmation

Now it starts to heat up in the kitchen. Some of the starry-eyed romance is giving way to the unspectacular reality. The couple is faced with the dilemma of self-revelation: They want to show more of their own secret selves, but they're afraid of rejection. Here, as they tentatively allow their courtship partner into their secret places and as they watch how the other person reacts, they start to become sure that this is (or isn't) *the one.*

During the process of confirmation, the couple learns how to overcome frustrations, jealousies, insecurities, and misunderstandings. This is the in-the-trenches phase of courtship. Many relationships do not survive it. But it's better for a couple to find out now that they're not compatible than in engagement or marriage.

Those couples who emerge from this phase still able to smile and gaze lovingly into each other's eyes are marvelously confirmed in their relationship. They now have actual evidence that their relationship isn't just built on bubbly infatuation. They have taken a close look at one another, seen the other person, warts and all, and still decided to remain committed.

This process doesn't end in marriage. There are some things that will never be revealed until two people actually live together. But the best that can be hoped for before then is a good, hard look at the other person. If the relationship can survive that, the couple has sufficient confidence in the expression of each other's love to declare the relationship publicly.

Phase Three: Engagement

The next logical step is for the man to approach the woman's father to ask for her hand in marriage. During this phase, the couple achieves a marriage of their souls that only awaits the calendar date.

So many marriages do not last. So many married couples have tension with one or both sets of in-laws. So many get into marriage before they really take a close look at their future spouse. All of these problems and more can be avoided through courtship.

READY FOR WEDDING BELLS?

Let's say you didn't know about courtship. Your teenager has been in a serious dating relationship for a long time, maybe years. They're talking about marriage. How can you know if they're ready? In this day of no-fault divorces and multiple marriages, you want your child's marriage to be able to withstand the fires of real life. So how can you know?

We believe that a couple is ready to consider marriage when they have reached maturity in three key areas: life-management skills, moral/social maturity, and compatibility discovery. Let's look at each one.

LIFE-MANAGEMENT SKILLS

A child is ready for marriage (or courtship) if he or she can manage basic life skills apart from Mom and Dad's supervision. A son or daughter must be able to handle the rigors of married life, including selfless care for another person. Both girls and boys must know how to prepare a meal, wash clothes, set a table, make wise purchases, manage finances, maintain employment that can sustain a family, and care for children.

Marriage is no place to start learning these basic life-management skills. Hopefully, you've been teaching these skills to your children all along.

MORAL/SOCIAL MATURITY

Among the most important developmental tasks to be achieved prior to marriage is the attainment of a moral/social maturity. Once a couple is married, neither one should be expecting to run home to Mommy when times get hard.

Before being ready for marriage, young people need to reach a level of social maturity that will allow them to function in an adult community. They need social adeptness in order to govern the dynamics of an adult relationship, especially a marital relationship. Think about your teenager: Does he or she behave like an adult in social settings? If not, better think about delaying the wedding.

Marriage will bring testing, conflicts, stress, and financial strain. No matter how long they've been courting or dating, there will always be an eye-opening period of discovery when each partner realizes things about the other that had so far remained concealed. There will be pressure from work, advice from in-laws, and obligations of responsible citizenship.

Marriage is hard. Immature young people need not apply.

COMPATIBILITY DISCOVERY

Many marriage problems result from couples not taking this component of marriage preparation seriously. Compatibility discovery is the process of investigating the proposed marriage partner to determine his or her suitability for marriage.

There are two noteworthy facts regarding marital compatibility. First, one does not *become* compatible with a mate. You're either compatible or you're not. True compatibility is discovered not learned.

Second, compatibility cannot be discovered if either party has not achieved basic life-management skills or moral/social maturity. A potential marriage partner who can't remember to pay bills or who expects Daddy to come and fix everything is not a compatible marriage partner for anyone.

THE SEVEN LEVELS OF COMPATIBILITY DISCOVERY

Stone quarries use gravel shakers to separate stones of various sizes. As crushed stone passes through smaller and smaller filters, each screen in a sense becomes the doorkeeper allowing passage for the purer and finer particles.

So it is with compatibility discovery in a couple. There are "compatibility screens" that allow or prevent deeper development in the relationship. As the two people pass through each screen, they grow closer and become more familiar and comfortable with their similarities and differences. If they decide to stop at any point, it would not destroy a friendship but would merely halt its progress at that level. These screens' purpose is to allow truly compatible couples to proceed with confidence and to halt ill-suited couples' progression toward a type of intimacy discovery reserved for marriage.

Level One: At-Large Social Compatibility

At-large social compatibility means the couple notices each other from a distance. Perhaps they see each other at a party or in class. They are simply attracted to one another.

Gary's son-in-law Paul and his daughter Jennifer first noticed each other while working together on a church project. Generally speaking, Jennifer and Paul had certain things in common. They were both committed to their church, they both enjoyed sports, and they were both active in youth ministry. It was in that public context that a general social compatibility was established.

It was a broad rapport, almost an absence of negatives rather than a presence of positives. Neither one did anything in public that caused the other to wish he or she were somewhere else. From a distance, they both recognized a general similarity that naturally encouraged them to move to the next level.

Level Two: General Personality Compatibility

It wasn't long after Paul and Jennifer met that they both realized how much they enjoyed working together. They appreciated each other's humor and moments of seriousness. Working together afforded them opportunities to witness the strengths and weaknesses of each other's personality. They found they enjoyed similar group projects, responded to certain situations the same way, and enjoyed many of the same leisure activities.

It was at this point that Jennifer and Paul began group dating. They would often go out with some of the youth leaders for meals after their ministry times.

Level Three: Friendship Compatibility

No male/female relationship should even begin leaning toward marriage until after a friendship has been established. Therefore courtship should not begin until a real friendship is present.

Jennifer and Paul discovered that they shared common values and goals. They enjoyed similar activities outside the context of youth work. They started doing fun little things for each other, such as when Paul shared his lunch when Jennifer forgot hers or when Jennifer baked Paul's favorite cookies for the all-boys weekend campout.

It was after they had developed this friendship compatibility that Paul approached Gary for permission to move to the first phase of courtship. He was doing more than asking to date his daughter: He was seeking approval to begin courting her, which meant he was wanting to investigate the possibility of marrying her. In so doing, they moved into the exploration phase of courtship (pp. 157–8).

If the relationship continued to progress, he would eventually need to come to Gary again to ask for her hand in marriage.

Level Four: Moral and Intellectual Compatibility

Once friendship compatibility is established, it quickly leads to the discovery of moral and intellectual compatibility, especially if the couple is in a courtship mode.

Not only did Jennifer and Paul enjoy similar fun activities while in each other's company, but they began to discover how each other viewed the world. That came by way of discovering each other's personal level of integrity and how each lived out his or her convictions. It also exposed their own intellectual skills as they discussed various issues of social and political theory and their general worldviews.

If there had been a major disagreement between them at this phase, something they could not seem to resolve no matter what, they might have decided to break off the courtship. Better to find out then that they were philosophically antithetical than to find out after the wedding. But their friendship would hopefully have remained.

Level Five: Family Compatibility

Couples are usually discovering family compatibility at the same time as they're discovering moral and intellectual compatibility. In this phase, each member of the couple is trying to see if there is a fit with the other's family.

During this time, Paul started to drop by the Ezzos' house more often. He participated in family nights, went out to dinner with them on occasion, and helped with a few household projects. The Ezzos were getting to know him as a family, and he was getting a glimpse into how things worked in Jennifer's family. By this time, too, Jennifer had become a household name with Paul's family.

It was at this point that Paul and Jennifer's relationship moved to the next level. It's a wonderful thing to see the man or woman of your dreams accepted heartily by your family. Paul approached Gary a second time to update him about how he and Jennifer were maturing in their love for one another. He voluntarily sought Gary's blessing to allow him to continue pursuing Jennifer, and Gary gave it.

Level Six: Private World Compatibility

It is at this level that one's capacity to be intimate is realized. Not physical intimacy, of course, but a type that is much more important for marriage: the intimacy of souls. During this phase each partner steps out to reveal his or her heart, complete with its fears and follies and moments of irrationality.

It's risky to be vulnerable to anyone, especially the person you may spend the rest of your life with. But when the other person treats you with compassion, you learn to trust, and you'll be likely to share further vulnerabilities later. There is nothing so wonderful as a marriage partner who knows you fully yet loves you anyway.

When Paul found that Jennifer could be trusted with his deepest fears and insecurities, and vice versa, they knew they were ready to commit to marriage. Paul came to Gary again and asked permission to continue pursuing Jennifer as his wife. If he was nervous about approaching Gary the first time, by the third time it was an easy thing.

Level Seven: Synergy Compatibility

In terms of marriage, synergy is present when the interaction of two individuals causes their life together to be greater than the sum of their lives apart. This phase isn't concerned so much with what the couple needs to discover about one another, but rather with what they realize about themselves as a team.

To succeed at this level, each should find that he or she is completed by the other. A husband should make his wife's endeavors far more successful than they were when she was on her own. A husband with a good wife will find himself capable of unimagined heights. That's synergy in a marriage. If it is not evident in the engagement, the couple needs to reconsider their plans. But if synergy is there, it's the final confirmation that the marriage will be what it is designed to be. Synergy compatibility allows the image of intimacy to be realized in its fullness.

It was at this point that Paul came to Gary a fourth time: to ask for Jennifer's hand in marriage. Five months later they were married.

Compatibility discovery is crucial before a couple says "I do." These seven layers of ever finer screens will ensure that problems are surfaced before vows are made—and, if no problems are identified during this time, a couple will gain great confidence to enter married life together.

STEPPING ON THE BRAKES

If at any point in the courtship, either member of the couple *or* either family had had misgivings about the relationship, they could have brought those up. That's the beauty of courtship over dating: There is a circle of advisors around the couple, people who can sometimes see things the person in the situation can't.

At one point in Jennifer and Paul's courtship, Jennifer began having hesitations about the relationship. With her parents support, Jennifer decided to take a month off. It was not an easy time for either Paul or Jennifer, but necessary. At the end of the month, Jennifer and Paul's love for each other was confirmed, and the courtship went forward at mach one.

We can probably all think of couples who got married but shouldn't have. If only they'd had the protection the courtship structure would have provided them. Your teen isn't just marrying the person he's dating, he's marrying that whole family. A courtship framework can prove the truth of the old saying, "In the abundance of counselors there is victory."

I'M SAVING MYSELF FOR MY WEDDING NIGHT

Throughout compatibility discovery, courtship or dating, and engagement, sexual purity is of greatest importance. Nothing can sabotage the marriage bed more effectively than guilt over premarital sex. And nothing is so beautiful as a pure man and woman coming together on their wedding night to consummate a marriage.

Though our society says a young man's not a man yet until he's had sex and a young woman who doesn't put out is a prude, it isn't so. That's just the voice of insecure people wanting others to validate their mistakes by repeating them. Encourage your teenager to remain sexually pure until marriage.

In a sense, even a young child is already married: He or she is promised to his or her future spouse. His or her wedding gift is remaining sexually pure for that person until the wedding night. Years before your child says "I do" at his or her wedding, he or she should have made sincere vows to that future bride or groom. It is an oath of faithfulness to remain sexually pure, given to the marriage partner in absentia.

How can you help your children succeed in this area? What can you do in a noncoercive way to encourage their purity and remind them of their pledge? Here is a beautiful example of how one father helped his daughter guard her heart for marriage and her future mate. While the daughter's age in this story is thirteen, other parents who have used this method have waited until their daughters were fifteen or sixteen.

On the occasion of her thirteenth birthday, a father planned a special date with his daughter. He wanted their time together to be so special that it would be almost impossible for his daughter to forget it. The father's purpose for the grand evening was to encourage her to commit herself to sexual purity during her teen years. He had planned this special date for months, and now everything was ready.

Early on the morning of the special day, the girl's mother presented her with a gold key, along with instructions to give the key as a gift to her father after he had given his gift to her. The mother assured her that she would then understand why she was to give away her birthday present.

That evening, the father arrived in a chauffeur-driven Mercedes to pick up his daughter. She was nervous about her first "date," but excited. The ride to the restaurant was filled with light, enjoyable conversation as father and daughter recounted many fun memories.

After a marvelous dinner, the father told his daughter that he wanted the very best for her life. He explained that she would be facing many new challenges in the years to come, one of which would be developing relationships with boys. He explained that, as her father, he had been given the joy and responsibility of watching over her and protecting her, especially during the teen years. Then he asked her to make a commitment that she would allow him to do that, to watch over her and protect her during her teen years.

At that moment, the father pulled out his gift and gave it to her. Inside, she found a beautiful gold heart on a gold chain. As the father placed the chain around her neck, he explained that the gold heart represented her sexual purity. He asked her if she had something for him. She remembered the key her mother had given her, and she brought it out. Before she could hand it to him, her father told her that by doing so she would be saying, "Yes, Dad, I want you to have the key to my heart, to protect it and keep it safe until marriage."

The father, understandably happy, made a promise to his little girl: "I will guard the key to your heart and all that it represents until the day of your wedding. Then I will give it to your husband."

If you have a son, you can adapt this ceremony for him. It's a little more complicated, but it accomplishes the same thing. After we describe our suggestion, you may be able to come up with a way that works better for you.

Use a woman's necklace and a man's ring for a boy. Mom and Dad take their son to dinner. Dad gives his son the necklace, which the boy then gives to the first woman in his life: his mother. She promises to keep it as a reminder of his pledge of purity and commitment to the girl who will someday be his wife. In exchange, Mom gives her son a gold ring engraved with the date of his pledge. The son is to wear the ring as a reminder of his vow of purity to his future wife.

On her son's wedding day, if the boy has abstained, the mother gives the necklace to the bride, symbolizing the fulfillment of his pledge. The son gives the ring to his father-in-law and mother-in-law, signifying his personal commitment to their daughter. (Or you could choose to use the ring in the construction of the wedding band.)

It is neither the ceremony nor the objects involved that assure commitment to these vows, but the steady, loving encouragement from Mom and Dad. Whether it be for a daughter or son, the locket, ring, and necklace are only reminders of a pledge. You are the most significant force in insuring that your child comes to his or her wedding in sexual purity.

SUMMARY

We don't believe it is best for teens to become involved in the dating experience outside of courtship. Dating, as it is usually defined today, can very often lead to improper intimacy, temporary relationships, and sexual experimentation, not to mention teenage pregnancy, AIDS, or abortion.

Not only is that not healthy for the person involved, it also defrauds the future mate. For too many teens, dating is like sampling a box of chocolates: They take a bite out of as many as they can, making them all undesirable for anyone who comes after.

In a sense, parents are custodians of their children. We are their managers or guardians. Think of someone who has been charged with delivering a custom-made car to its new owner. It seems **the** world itself rises up to damage that car: Rust, flying pebbles, salt air, other cars, criminals, and paint-scratching delinquents all work to spoil the beauty of what you're handling. So it is your task to give that car defenses against the elements and protect it from those who would hurt it so that you can present it to its rightful owner in pristine condition.

Instill in your teenager a passion for purity—purity in his or her own body and a demand for purity in the life of his or her future mate.

BRINGING IT HOME

1. How do you feel about letting your teenager date? What restrictions, if any, do you feel are appropriate?

2. Do you think courtship, as the authors described it, is too radical for your family? What elements of the idea of courtship would you like to incorporate for your own teen?

3. What is the primary difference between dating and courtship, and how do you feel about it?

4. What are the three phases of courtship?

5. What, if anything, would you add to the authors' list of what a teen must display before being ready for marriage?

Special Resource Section

Chapter Ten

One-Stop Q & A Guide to the Teen Years

POPULARITY, PEER PRESSURE, AND SELF-IMAGE

- My teenager is starting to hang around with the wrong crowd. What can I do?
- My teenager would do anything to be accepted by the group. Should I be worried?
- My teenager is very popular in school, but I'm getting reports that he (or she) is unkind to those not in the right clique. Is it my place to say anything?
- My teenager is not the most attractive or popular person in school. She tries to be accepted by the popular kids, but they only ridicule her. What can I do?
- My daughter doesn't think I notice, but I'm beginning to suspect she's got an eating disorder. How can I be sure? What can I do to help?

SCHOOL

- Public schools are getting so violent. Should I put my teenager in a private school?
- My teenager is tormented so badly by other kids at school that it's a struggle just to get him (or her) to go. What can I do?

COLLEGE AND CAREER

- My teenager is so unmotivated in school now, why should I believe things will be different in college? Why should I spend money I don't have to send an unmotivated teen to college?
- My teenager wants to go into professional sports (or into a career in the arts), but I don't think he's got the talent to make it. How do I get him to think realistically without squashing his dreams?
- What guidelines can you give me about jobs—full-time, part-time, after-school, and summer jobs?

THE OPPOSITE SEX AND SEXUAL EXPERIMENTATION

- I'm pretty sure my teenager is sexually active. What should I do?
- I'm afraid to leave my teenager at home when I'm gone, especially overnight, for fear of what will go on while I'm away. What should I do?
- I found a pornographic magazine in my son's room. Should I confront him about it?
- I'm afraid my teenager is more interested in same-gender sexual experimentation than any other kind. What can I do?

- My daughter is pregnant, and the father doesn't want the baby. What should I do?
- My daughter has had an abortion. Now all she does is cry. What can I say that will help?

DRUGS AND ALCOHOL

- By the time my child was eight, he'd been confronted with drugs, guns, sex, pornography, theft, alcohol, and homosexuality. Do you think this is why he struggles so much as a teenager?
- My teenager is a good kid. I don't have to worry about drugs or alcohol, do I?
- I'm thinking that my teenager should try a little of everything, just to see what it's all about. That way it's easier to know if something should be accepted or rejected. Is this a good plan?

REBELLION

- I didn't discover your books until too late. My teenager is in complete rebellion. I'm so afraid and angry and hurt. What can I do?
- My teenager won't even talk to me. How can I work on the great communication suggestions you make in this book?
- My teenager is showing signs that he doesn't respect me anymore. What can I do to regain my authority?
- My teenager doesn't openly defy me but rather pushes the limit a bit. If I say be home by ten, she's home at ten-fifteen. Do I have grounds to be upset?

- My teenager came home with a certain part of his (or her) body pierced. What can I do?

DISCIPLINE AND CONTROL

- My teenager gets angry when I ask him (or her) to do chores around the house. What can I do to feel like I'm still in charge in this home? (Am I still in charge?)
- When he's with me, my teenager is well behaved. It's when he's not with me that worries me. How can I be sure he's acting properly when I'm not around?
- When I try to discipline my teen, he just gets into his car and drives off.

VIOLENCE AND CRIME

- Although I can't prove it, I suspect my teenager has broken the law, perhaps more than once. I don't want to turn my own child in to the police. What should I do?
- Ever since my husband and I got divorced, our teenager has been acting out violently. How can I help if reconciliation is not an option?
- My teenager has mentioned suicide a few times. Should I take it seriously?
- My twelve-year-old son has drugged me numerous times and tried to kill me. I'm not kidding. I can't live like this anymore. Help! He also leaves the pool gate open purposely, hoping to encourage our three-year-old daughter to go for a swim at the bottom of the pool. He has admitted his motives. I've worked through *Preteen Wise* and a host of other books and

courses. What can I do short of having him arrested and taken from our home?

THE MEDIA

- I'm so fed up with my teenager's media choices that I'm just about ready to cancel cable, throw away the TV and the radio, break some CDs, and sell our computer. Before I go on my rampage, is there a better way to react?
- My teenager plays video games from the moment he gets home from school until I force him to go to bed at night. I'm thinking things are a little out of control. Am I crazy, or could he be addicted to that thing?

SPIRITUALITY

- My daughter has gotten into Wicca. Is this just pretend, more like a girl's club than anything serious, or should I be concerned?
- My teenager has begun hearing voices and acting strangely, sometimes like someone else entirely. Is this just hormones, or should I be concerned? Should I see somebody about this? If so, who?
- I don't want to impose my own beliefs or values on my teenager. I want him to find his own spiritual path. How can I help with that?
- My teenager says she's become a Buddhist. Does a parent have any say over that sort of thing?

In this special section, we've put together answers to many questions parents of teenagers are asking. We hope you will find it a valuable resource.

Of course, we are not in your home. We can only give general answers. Sometimes they will not apply in your situation. Our hope is that we can at least get you in the neighborhood of something that will help. The principles we use should fit your situation even if the specifics don't.

Also, all parents are at different places in their parenting. Some people on the rapport/conflict scale we introduced in chapter 1 have it pretty easy. Their biggest problem is they can't get their teen to turn off the lights in his bedroom. Other people are dealing with more grave matters: drugs, sexual activity, crime. Again, we believe the principles we present here can be scaled up or down to fit most situations.

POPULARITY, PEER PRESSURE, AND SELF-IMAGE

My teenager is starting to hang around with the wrong crowd. What can I do?

The reason we never think our kids are hanging around with a bad crowd when they're in third or fourth grade is that those kids didn't look so bad back then. They seemed pretty normal, though perhaps not particularly well behaved. Now, when those same kids are sixteen or seventeen, we wonder how we could have missed it. Your child may be hanging around with the very same kids, only now you see the glaring moral disparity that was almost invisible before.

We get nervous when we look at these kids and see the signs of where some of them may be headed in terms of the trouble they could potentially get into. We know we don't want our kids to get there. But from the child's perspective, nothing's changed. These are still the same kids they've always hung around with.

Any approach you take to attempt to lead your teen away from these peers must rely on the power of your relationship with your teen. You need to sit down and have an honest talk about the types of behavior that are right for your family. If your family has established a common moral stance, you can appeal to that. Point out some of the more dangerous aspects of particular lifestyles. Hopefully, your teen will agree with you that there is a disparity between what those friends are like and what your family stands for and will see the need to make a break.

But don't do it in time of crisis. When your teen says, "Mom, can I go over to Matt's house today because we're going to spend the weekend together?" that's not the time to say, "No, I don't like Matt." Your timing is probably as important in these conversations as the words you use. When talking about any important issue with your teen, make sure you operate in periods of nonconflict.

Keep the concept of substitution over suppression in mind (see chapter 6). If you're going to attempt to suppress a relationship, make sure you're ready to substitute something in its place. If you're going to tell your teen that these are not the best kids for her to hang around with, you'd better be establishing relationships with families that have great kids. Provide a natural alternative. You simply can't cut off relationships with your kids without providing them with a substitution.

Sit down with your teen and have a talk. Ask her what qualities draw her to these friends. Then ask how she feels these qualities and these friends are going to help her reach her goals in life. As kids get into the teen years, you want them to come to their own conclusions. You provide guidance, but you don't make the decisions for them. It's so much better for your teen to say, "Yeah, maybe this guy really isn't the best one for me to hang around with," than for you to dictate that to her. When your teen realizes for herself that someone is a bad influence, she'll be more willing to break off that relationship. But if you dictate with your authority, you're just asking for strife.

My teenager would do anything to be accepted by the group. Should I be worried?

Sometimes it's a good thing to want to be accepted by the group. Peer pressure isn't always bad. If it's a positive group, with values you agree with, then it may be applying positive peer pressure on your child. He may clean up some behaviors just because of his new friends.

There are personality, temperament, and love language variables that may make your teenager predisposed to want to be accepted or close to a group. However, if you're pretty sure that isn't the case with your teen, you should try to determine what it is that is motivating him to want so badly to be accepted by this group. We all need to feel accepted and appreciated. But if a teen is willing to do nearly anything to be accepted, it may be cause for alarm. Help your teenager evaluate exactly why this is so important in his life that he's willing to compromise who he is to be accepted by them.

You may find that this is really a need for more time with Dad or an indication that you've got an independent family as opposed to an interdependent one (see chapter 5). Or there may be some deficiency in the child's self-perception. If he feels his own identity will be enhanced by just being friends with these people, then you as his parent need to deal with the root issue (the lack he feels in his own self) rather than the symptoms.

My teenager is very popular in school, but I'm getting reports that he (or she) is unkind to those not in the right clique. Is it my place to say anything?

It's always your place as a mom and dad to be a moral compass. This behavior, if true, calls for correction. In chapter 6 we talked about how correction simply means "putting back on track." This situation does not necessarily call for discipline. It may be more appropriate to provide moral correction. Point out how his actions may be hurting others. Consider using a Nathan parable.

Isn't it wonderful that your teenager is well accepted? If you have a child like this, you have the opportunity to instill graciousness and empathy. Teach your popular teen to reach out in kindness and gentleness to those who don't have everything he has. A teen who is friendly to those who are less popular is attractive in a way that transcends nice looks, clothes, and teeth.

My teenager is not the most attractive or popular person in school. She tries to be accepted by the popular kids, but they only ridicule her. What can I do?

Usually when your teen desires acceptance by a certain group, it's saying more about your teen than about the group. The key question is why your teen feels she has to be accepted by this particular group. Sit down and talk with her. Ask her what it is this group offers that she desires. What would she gain if she were accepted by this group, and what would it mean about her if she weren't? Listen for clues about what she feels she's lacking that she thinks this group would provide. That's where you should focus your efforts to help your daughter.

The hard truth is that life is not fair. Not everyone will like your child. Young people can be terribly cruel to one another. If this group is rejecting your daughter, it may also be because of insecurities of their own, because confident people welcome new friends easily.

Take this opportunity to gently teach your child. Rejection hurts. Right now, she's feeling like the outcast. But that won't always be the case. Help her to understand that she will often be in a position of accepting or rejecting others. Now that she knows how awful rejection feels, she can determine to reach out to others in the future. Have her seek friends from outside the "in group." She may find that there are more neat kids outside the in group than inside.

My daughter doesn't think I notice, but I'm beginning to suspect she's got an eating disorder. How can I be sure? What can I do to help?

Eating disorders are serious business. There are specialists in this area who can give you information that will allow you to evaluate and attempt to understand the problem. There is also good information available on the Internet. The first step is to get educated. If, after you've learned a bit, your suspicions seem to be confirmed, consider taking her to a specialist.

Eating disorders usually have at their root a sense that the young person has failed to be accepted by people who are close to her, especially her father. If your daughter is showing signs of an eating disorder, Dad needs to get more involved, if at all possible. It is amazing what one bicycle ride, one walk in the park, or one trip to the mall with Dad can do for a daughter who is developing symptoms of any of these disorders.

Dad, pick up a copy of *On Becoming Preteen Wise* and read the chapter called "The Father's Mandate." That chapter illustrates a child's need for a healthy relationship with Dad and gives practical ideas for how to build one with your children.

In a case like this, parents need to concentrate on purposefully expressing their unconditional acceptance of their teen. If they realize they *haven't* been extending unconditional acceptance, then that's where they need to start working.

SCHOOL

Public schools are getting so violent. Should I put my teenager in a private school?

We often hear the sentiment that public schools are terrible, private schools are better (but expensive), and homeschooling is the "safest" option (though not without problems of its own). But this isn't true across the board. There are some wonderful public schools, some scary private schools, and some unhealthy home-school situations.

The number one consideration for moms and dads is their teen's health and safety. Until we come to a place in our society where we have a common level of human decency and protection for all, we are going to be faced with hostility in some public schools. If you or your teen feel he is not safe where he is, consider making a change.

Because of the tragedies in several public schools, many parents are considering private schools for their kids. But these can be expensive, and they're not right for every teen. If your teen goes to a private school, she may have to give up a lot of great activities and sports that are offered at the public school. On the other hand, the student-to-teacher ratios are usually better at private schools, and they tend to give more attention to character.

Homeschooling might be an option to consider. This movement, once popular primarily among Evangelical Christians, has now become quite fashionable in the mainstream culture. However, as with private schools, homeschooling isn't for everyone. It's a lot of work for parents, not all of whom feel they can adequately teach their children, especially at the high school level. And let's face it, not all parents want to have their teenagers around them that much.

Talk to your own teenager about the issue. Some teens will say, "Yes, please get me out of this school." They recognize the struggle that's going on, and they actually would not mind being homeschooled. That might sound like a foreign concept, but we've met some teens who were willing to move out of a public school just because of the violence they were seeing around them.

The good news is this doesn't have to be a once-for-all decision. It's sometimes a good idea to try all three—homeschool until age seven, for instance, private school through ninth grade, then public school until graduation, or some other arrangement. Keep tinkering with your options until you find what's right for your teen and your family at this time. Evaluate it every semester.

My teenager is tormented so badly by other kids at school that it's a struggle just to get him (or her) to go. What can I do?

Kids who have been raised morally are often attractive targets for those who have not been raised that way. Living according to a high moral standard will always make a teen stand out. It can become very uncomfortable when the culture of the school militates against what a teen stands for.

What can you do about this? Well, you're certainly not going to *not* teach your teen to be responsible or respectful or moral simply to avoid ridicule. You must give your teen confidence and tools for dealing with this kind of harassment. You may also want to evaluate whether your teen is in the right school situation for this time in her life.

This scenario demonstrates the need both for a strong family identity and for a moral community. These will give him the ability to resist peer pressure and will give him some like-minded friends to stand with in the struggle.

COLLEGE AND CAREER

My teenager is so unmotivated in school now, why should I believe things will be different in college? Why should I spend money I don't have to send an unmotivated teen to college?

A lack of motivation in school may be a behavior problem or it may not. Some temperaments have a greater desire to please and achieve than others. We don't want you to feel that if you have an unmotivated teen that you're a terrible parent. One of us (Gary Ezzo) gave his parents a very hard time because he was simply unmotivated when it came to school. If he wanted to do something, he had all the motivation in the world. But if someone else wanted him to do something, he wasn't interested.

Gary says: "My family had two apple trees. Every year there was one Saturday when my brother and I had to rake up the apples that had made it through the winter but had fallen in springtime and begun to rot on the ground. My brother had no problem doing this chore. He would just take that rake and get the job done. But I had a tree, too. I just didn't want to rake those apples. There were other things in life I really wanted to do besides rake apples. So I would just wait it out.

"I have to say I don't think my parents handled this situation correctly, because I knew that if I didn't rake those apples, someone would eventually come and do it for me. I was more motivated to ride it out than to do the work even though it wouldn't have taken me fifteen minutes to do it."

Believe it or not, there still are children like that. If you've got one and you're considering whether or not you should send him to college, you should make sure your expectations are realistic. Whether your teen is unmotivated because of temperament or behavioral deficiencies, the results may be the same. Some parents choose to allow their teenagers to wait on college until they've gotten some direction for their lives and proven their willingness to help pay their way through school.

The key for parents of an unmotivated teen is not to try to

break him of this but to find out what it is that does motivate him. Draw from the unique giftedness and personality of the teen to find the secret for getting him moving. If you can tap into that, the motivation problems may disappear.

Or you can always try to scare your teenager straight by giving him a dose of what life without a college education might be like. You can teach tomorrow's consequences today. That's what Gary's parents did.

"My folks worked in a shoe factory. When each of us boys turned sixteen, we lost the privilege of having summers off from school. We had to go to work. The summer after my sixteenth birthday I had to follow my brother.

"Of course there was no air conditioning in that factory. The room we worked in was over a hundred degrees. My job was to go into another room, which was about 120 degrees inside, where there was this large oil pool in which the pieces of shoe leather would soak. I would jump into that oil well and pull the leather out. (This was before OSHA had a lot of fancy guidelines.)

"I did this all summer long. Every evening I would drag myself out to my parents' Chevy to wait for them. I would nearly pass out on the seat I was so exhausted. Every night, Dad would get in, look at me in the rearview mirror, and say, 'How was work today, son?' I would say fine. And every day my dad would say, 'You will go to college, or you will do this the rest of your life.'"

If your teen is unmotivated for college, consider putting her into a vocation. Give her a job before you send money off to school. It may be that she never goes to college. There is a misconception that if your kids don't go to college, they won't be able to make it in life. But we know many people who never went to college and are making more money than most Ph.D.'s.

My teenager wants to go into professional sports (or into a career in the arts), but I don't think he's got the talent to make it. How do I get him to think realistically without squashing his dreams?

This is a tough one. You have to handle your child's dreams with care. But you also want to equip him to succeed in life.

Sometimes the problem will solve itself. After a season of interest in music or hockey or whatever, your teen may decide he's not that interested after all. But if your teen is nearing the end of high school and is talking about pursuing the art or sport through college and beyond, it might be time for parents to gently intervene.

First, be sure you evaluate your child accurately. Get the opinion of others qualified to judge. If there really is unusual talent there, you may actually want to step up your support of the activity. If there is only a moderate amount of talent, you may want to begin thinking about other paths he might take. If there is raw talent but no determination to excel, your teen doesn't have a chance of making it. He would be better off coming to grips with that now rather than later.

Consider giving your teen the opportunity to investigate an activity. Let him play for a season or do repertory theater for a summer. If, after a fair time of investigation, your teen hasn't demonstrated the requisite talent level or commitment, you need to help him face the reality that this may not be for him, at least not as a career.

Even with talent and determination, it's very often not enough to make it in careers in sports and the arts. Free agent tryouts in pro sports and open auditions in the performing arts are overflowing with talented and determined people. Gifted, trained, and experienced players and performers are a dime a dozen. There will usually be twenty people more qualified than your child for every available spot.

We think our schools, especially our high schools, do children a disservice by giving unreserved encouragement in the areas of sports and the arts. Teenagers are trying to figure out what they want to do in life. If they excel in basketball or dance, teachers and parents will encourage them to pursue it in college. They communicate the message that the young person "has what it takes" to make it in this field as a career, when in actuality what this teen may have is the talent to stand out at the high school level. High school standout talent is not the same as successful career talent.

So these teens go to college where, not surprisingly, there are degree plans in sports and fine arts (often taught by former high school standouts who didn't have the ability to make a career out of doing it and so have turned to teaching). The young adult graduates from college having played on the team or with a degree in vocal performance or theater...and finds he can't get a job. After disappointing tryouts in Green Bay or off Broadway, he begins to realize the hard truth.

Perhaps he thinks back to all those teachers and professors who encouraged him along the way and wonders why they didn't tell him this would happen instead of always painting lovely but unlikely pictures. Here he sits with no marketable skills and a degree no one values. How is he going to support himself?

Parents want to encourage their children, and so they should. We want them to be confident and realize they have something special to offer. But we should also want to help them survive in this harsh, sometimes cruel, world.

Here is the key for handling this difficult situation. In order to encourage your child to follow her dream and yet still be sure she'll be able to support herself if the dream never becomes reality, *develop a contingency plan with your teen.*

Say something along these lines: "Son, you really are gifted in this activity. Your father and I want to help you learn your craft and take advantage of every opportunity to turn this into your career if that's what you want. But we also want you to be able to take care of yourself while you're waiting for your big break. So, alongside the classes you take to hone your skills in this area, we want you to take classes in computer programming or accounting or business management, something that will help you get a well-paying job to support you while you work to make your dreams come true."

With a plan like this, you can show your support of your child's aspirations and also be sure she is taken care of over the long haul.

What guidelines can you give me about jobs—full-time, part-time, after-school, and summer jobs?

There are two primary scenarios when it comes to teens and jobs: They either want one or they don't. Here are some guidelines for both situations.

If your teen wants a job, be it an after-school job or a summer job, the first question to ask is why she wants it. Is it for money or status or approval? What is the money going to go for? Is she hoping to earn some extra cash to fund her CD-buying habit or is she saving up to move away from you? Do you think the money will go for pizza or for drugs? Is there a rebellion issue at play? If so, that needs to be what you address first.

Jobs can be great teachers for the real world. You can use a job to help your teen learn how to manage money, how to be a responsible employee, and how to value a dollar. In real life, if you don't work, you don't have money to spend. An after-school or summer job can help drive this home. It can be an excellent way to transfer some more monkeys onto your teen's back. He can begin to assume responsibility for his own clothing purchases, car fuel and upkeep, and whatever extras he desires.

The second question you need to ask is whether a job would be the best use of your teen's time. If it's a summer job, would summer school serve her better? If working on a skill or sport might give her a better chance of receiving a scholarship, maybe a job wouldn't be the best option right now.

Third, will this job interfere with schoolwork, family time, or other responsibilities? If the cost is higher than the family is willing to pay, it might be better to wait on the job. You might consider just trying it for a while to see if the benefits outweigh the costs. If it turns out that they don't, you can reevaluate.

The second scenario is when the teen doesn't want a job, but Mom and Dad want him to get one. Teens work hard during the school year, often taking on sports and arts and other extracurricular activities that can add up to sixty-plus hours of activity a week. When summertime comes, they can want to just crash for two months before starting it all over again.

We understand. However, in the real world, they're not going to get nice two-month vacations every year. If they're lucky, they'll get a week. After they've been there twenty years, maybe they'll work up to three weeks in a year. Allowing teens to have such a big vacation does not do them any favors in terms of equipping them for life.

That doesn't mean your teen doesn't need a vacation. Try to incorporate some rejuvenation time into the summer. Maybe allow a week or two break between school and the job. If she can find a job with flexible hours or in which she'll be doing something she enjoys, so much the better. It's a balance. Help out by discussing the options and laying out parameters.

One mother told her teenage son he had to get a summer job working at least twenty hours a week. When he moaned about it, she gave him another option. "Okay, you don't have to get a job; you can work for me. I'll give you at least twenty hours of work every week. But I only pay twenty-five cents an hour." Needless to say, he was motivated to go find a part-time job.

Jobs can be wonderful tools for parents to teach hard lessons about what makes the world go 'round.

THE OPPOSITE SEX AND SEXUAL EXPERIMENTATION

I'm pretty sure my teenager is sexually active. What should I do?

The answer to this question will depend on your own moral position and on how premarital sex is viewed in your home. Some parents just simply expect that the normal course of adolescence will lead their teenager into some type of sexual experimentation.

Other parents may not consider this a moral wrong but simply as a way for children to express themselves. Teenage pregnancy and sexually transmitted diseases—not to mention the emotional damage done when a sexual relationship is broken off—are considered unfortunate but hardly unexpected consequences. These parents will probably not interfere with their child's sexual activity.

Still other parents, usually those operating from a Judeo-Christian worldview, consider sex outside of marriage to be a moral wrong. If your child is sexually active and this goes against your family's moral consensus, you need to consider what forces may be at work that would cause your child to go against the family. Is there a legitimate need that this illegitimate activity is meeting?

With daughters, premature sexual experimentation usually happens because she hasn't had enough Daddy time. If you think this might be true of your daughter, you'll probably not be able to fix the problem by saying, "Stay away from that boy." You'd do better to handle this problem not with suppression but with substitution.

If Dad is in the home, he needs to spend more time with his daughter. He needs to find appropriate ways to physically touch her, maybe even hold her in his lap. The only reason she's looking to be held and touched by boys is because she's not being held and touched by Daddy. It's a legitimate need. She probably doesn't even like the sexual aspect of it; that's just the price she has to pay to get the simple physical affection and personal attention she craves.

Dad, touch your daughter. Give her hugs. Take her on dates. Spend unstructured time with her, just talking. You're forming in her the image of what she will expect from a husband.

It shouldn't just be parents from the Judeo-Christian world-view who develop practices that help their children maintain the integrity of their own bodies. If you desire that your daughter have a healthy marriage, then these practices should interest you, whether you're a religious person or not. Teenagers who engage in multiple sexual experiences before marriage go on to have the highest divorce rate.

A son from a morally conservative home who is sexually active is usually trying to establish a feeling of masculinity. The guys in the locker room ask if he's a real man yet. Sometimes that can tap into a young man's insecurities, causing him to want to prove that, yes, he's got what it takes to be manly. And so he goes looking for a girl who needs to receive the affections of a father-surrogate, and together they make a mess.

A son's lack of confidence in his own masculinity also stems from a deficiency of Daddy time. If there is no father around to show him that being a man is more about gentleness and devotion than it is about sexual prowess, then a teenage boy defaults to what his peers tell him being a man means. And, since most of those peers who are talking about it don't know what being a man really means either, there's another mess in the making. There is nothing so wonderful for a child than an engaged, loving father.

But what do you do if you're a single mom? What happens to the morality and purity you're trying to instill into your teen if he's with Dad every other weekend, Dad has a live-in girlfriend, and there's pornography all over the place? What happens to the teen's discipline when the father takes the role of Disneyland Dad and lets the teenager do whatever he wants when he's there?

If you suspect your son or daughter is sexually active, you need to have an honest conversation. Hopefully this won't be the first such talk you've had with your child about sex. If so, you (not your child) may not be ready for it. But you've got to do it anyway.

Susan's husband went out of town for a business trip, so Susan thought it would be the perfect opportunity to talk to her fourteen-year-old son, Michael. Susan planned the whole evening: She made Michael's favorite dinner and rented a movie for them to watch afterwards. After dinner, she began to tentatively probe into the issue of his sexuality. She found she was having more trouble actually getting to the point than she thought she would.

After a few of his mother's awkward tries, Michael said, "Mom, is this the sex talk we're supposed to have?"

"How did you know?"

"Well, when I saw your eyes darting back and forth from the ceiling to the wall and that you never looked at me, I figured this must be it."

Some families can talk about sex more easily than others. Just remember that you don't have to discover the mother lode of information all at once. Plan on spreading this investigation of yours over the next three weeks or three months or six months. Needing to know all the details right away only shows your fear. If you come on that way, your teen may clam up, because he thinks you're trying to snoop into his private life. Not only will you not find out what you want to know, you also run the risk of damaging your teen's trust.

The key to dealing with your child's sexual activity will always be dialogue. If there's no father in the house or if it wouldn't work for you to have this conversation, perhaps you can find someone else the teenager respects who can sit down and talk to him in place of Dad. Maybe it's someone in his twenties who was sexually active in his teens but now realizes the devastation that came from that. The worst thing to do is to just let it go and ignore it. Somehow, little by little, you've got to bring it up and discuss it with your teen. Just let her know that you're open to conversation on this topic.

I'm afraid to leave my teenager at home when I'm gone, especially overnight, for fear of what will go on while I'm away. What should I do?

Until you get some things under control, you may just not be able to leave your teen at home alone. If you think your son will have a wild party or your daughter will have a boy over, then you just can't provide that opportunity. If you have to be gone, send him to relatives.

Better yet, take him with you. Use that time together as a chance to work on your relationship. Employ the principles we give in this book until your teen has regained respect for you and you have regained trust in your teen.

I found a pornographic magazine in my son's room. Should I confront him about it?

Your son has been exploited. His natural masculine propensities have been ill-used to make a buck. In our culture, human sexuality is not usually portrayed as something beautiful and reserved for marriage. It's depicted as an object to be marketed and sold—or as a tool to market and sell something else. Pornography is so plentiful in our land because there is a financial market that supports it.

Parents, particularly mothers, need to understand that pornography is addictive, every bit as addictive as crack cocaine. It takes what is good and healthy and perverts it. Then it won't let go. That's why you're not going to be able to just take the magazine away, give your son a stern talking to, and be done with it forever. It's gained a foothold in his heart and has to be dealt with as a heart issue.

One argument we've heard trying to justify looking at pornography is that technically, no one's getting hurt. The pictures are already there on the page, so how is anyone getting hurt? Well, the person looking at the pornography is getting hurt, for one. He's creating conditions within his own mind and imagination that will be replayed over and over again, haunting him.

Like a drug, the level of pornography that once satisfied quickly ceases to satisfy, so the user goes to the next level. Deeper and deeper he sinks into the most abominable hard-core porn. In short order, a young man's mind can become so debauched as to almost be unrecoverable.

Pity the new wife who comes to her wedding night in purity, expecting to be treated with gentleness and honor, only to find that her husband expects a brand of sexual activity that would make a prostitute blush. Ask her if she thinks pornography hurts others.

Pornography hurts the people in the magazine. How many times do we hear women, particularly celebrities, say how terribly they regret posing for such pictures? It's almost become a joke: "I was young and I needed the money." Pornography damages the models' reputations, sense of privacy, and self-worth. The more magazines that sell, the more demand there will be to victimize other young girls—maybe your daughter—in this way.

And pornography hurts young people. As the demand for pornographic material rises—elevated, in part, by whoever purchased the magazine in your son's room—the pornographic industry flourishes, reaching more and more innocent eyes and hearts. Those who market this material know that it is like a drug, and that free samples given out will almost surely result in paying customers.

Don't assume this is just a problem with your son. Do some self-evaluation about the atmosphere of sexuality in your home. If you are regularly inviting R-rated movies into your house, for instance, movies with nudity and simulated sex, then a pornographic magazine is just the logical next step for your son. Is this issue important enough to you as a family that you're willing to stop bringing that type of entertainment into your house? Consider setting a moral standard for your family, beginning with a determination not to bring in movies that have sexually explicit or even suggestive scenes. There are movie guides and on-line sites that review movies for offensive content.

If the family environment has created the hunger for pornography in your son, then the family environment may have to change. You're not going to sit there in front of what is really a quasi-pornographic movie, then tell your son not to look at "that trashy magazine." It won't fly.

If you've found pornography in your son's room, you need to take it very seriously. You will want to confront him about it, but if you're feeling angry or betrayed, you've got to wait until you've cooled down. Come at it during a period of nonconflict. If you come in anger, you're going to shut the teenager down right there, and you're not going to get anywhere.

Remember that boys are wired to find the female form attractive. That's not to justify pornography, but for you to realize that this is just a perversion of something that is natural and good. If you think about it that way, it should help you calm down enough to talk about it.

Then don't confront your son directly. In *On Becoming Preteen Wise,* we pointed out the differences in how boys and girls handle confrontation. Girls tend to do better with direct confrontation ("Can we talk?"), while boys tend to do better with indirect confrontation.

So plan to discuss this with your son while you're doing something else. Maybe you can watch a football game on TV and talk about it between plays. Maybe you can talk about it when you're working on the car or cooking dinner. Guys sometimes like to have something else to stare at when they talk about matters of the heart because eye contact can be too intense.

You may not even have to bring the topic up directly. Just bring it up generally and see if your son gets the drift. If you talk about it in generalities or about some hypothetical person somewhere, you may give him the chance to surrender with dignity rather than pushing him into a corner.

This would be a great opportunity to employ a Nathan parable (see chapter 6). Set up a fictional scenario, maybe using an addictive drug as what the person is experimenting with. Ask your son to comment about why he thinks this person should or shouldn't continue with the drug. It's a great feeling when you see someone prescribing his own solution. When you finally reveal that he is the person in the story and the drug they're really talking about is pornography, you'll see that teaching go straight into his heart. It may not work right away, but you've certainly made your point (he's made it for you, actually), and you know that he's heard you loud and clear.

Sometimes men, even teens, can desire to be free of pornography but not know how to win free. There are good books in your bookstore and helpful sites on-line that can help. Treat this like you would any addiction.

I'm afraid my teenager is more interested in same-gender sexual experimentation than any other kind. What can I do?

The debate as to whether or not there is a natural, genetic sexual orientation will continue for many years. To date we have not seen conclusive evidence, in spite of all the claims, that there is a genetically determined sexual orientation. Homosexuality has nothing to do with genetics, nor even with sex. It has everything to do with relationships.

From the time of Freud to the present day, the preponderance of evidence indicates that homosexual tendencies are the result of two things: a son punishing his father for a form of abuse and a lack of a father relationship (this is often the case even with lesbians). Also, families with a dominant mother and passive father tend to generate children with homosexual inclinations more than other kinds of families do. Once again we see the importance of a strong, involved, loving father.

In every society, we see gender predispositions that are so uniform they must be determined by genes. It's no accident that the little guy down in Texas will pick up a stick and shoot all the bad guys and the little Arawak boy in a South American rain forest will pick up a spear and pretend to throw it at enemies. There is a natural propensity within the masculine psyche to be dominant, to be the protector. In the same way, there is a natural propensity for girls to nurture and comfort and build relationships. Homosexuality is not a naturally occurring phenomenon.

Parents should always be encouraging their children toward their gender predispositions. As we have said, young people who are leaning toward homosexuality are usually doing so because of a deficiency in how they have been fathered. We believe that as the divorce rate continues to rise and fathers continue to flee the home, homosexuality will increase.

Sometimes parents can get concerned if their younger boy seems to appreciate things that are considered more "feminine." Parents may see their son out picking flowers or playing dress-up and fear he has a tendency towards homosexuality. That is not the case. It may, in fact, say more about the parents than about the child.

Young children are discovering their world. They see someone do something, particularly a parent or older sibling, and they want to try it for themselves. Imitation is how all children learn. A boy who likes picking flowers may just be expressing an appreciation for beauty. If in a few years he brings the flowers he picks to a young girl, she will be most pleased and not think he's effeminate at all. A young girl who likes to play with tractors and climb trees may just be displaying management potential or enjoying feeling strong. Watch out for this girl in the basketball courts and office buildings in a few years.

If parents are disturbed by their child's "wrong gender" behavior, perhaps they need to examine themselves. What is the harm of a girl who can throw a fastball and a boy who moves with grace? "Wrong gender" attributes like these aren't wrong at all. It's very fashionable for a girl to be athletic, and the best male athletes move with fluidity.

Usually it is the "man's man" type of father who is uncomfortable with a son who doesn't chew nails and beat up on little kids. Is there, perhaps, an insecurity in the father's own sense of masculinity? There is the possibility that this little guy's temperament and personality just make him a more sensitive kid. If the father sends fearful messages demanding that the boy be more manly, he can unwittingly cause his child to lean more toward effeminate behavior as he grows. This is what we mean when we say homosexuality can be a way for a child to punish his father for a kind of abuse. He wants to know if his father's love is unconditional or if it will only be given out if he acts a certain way.

If you have a young child who seems interested in things that traditionally belong in the other gender's realm of activity, relax. Just realize that this is most likely simply an experiment. If you don't charge the activity with emotional electricity, your child will probably grow tired of it soon and move on to something else, just as he or she has tried and discarded countless other games, songs, and activities. Rest in the knowledge that if there is healthy fathering going on in your child's life, he or she will naturally grow into a confident man or woman.

My daughter is pregnant, and the father doesn't want the baby.
What should I do?

The key question everyone needs to be asking is what would be best for the unborn child. Every child deserves a mother and a father. If you as this child's biological grandparents are unable or unwilling to raise this baby, then we would heartily encourage you to urge your daughter to put her baby up for adoption.

There are many organizations that deal with this: crisis pregnancy centers, churches, adoption agencies, and other social services. They can answer your questions and help connect you with the resources you need. It's important that you and your daughter understand all the options.

Every situation is different. For some, adoption is clearly the best choice. There are a lot of husbands and wives in our country who cannot have children and would be wonderful parents for this baby. There are situations in which the biological mother can raise the child with the support and help of loving grandparents. Other times the father might have a genuine change of heart and desire to marry your daughter and raise this child as his own. That might or might not be the best solution.

Keep the main thing in focus: What is in the best interest of this baby?

My daughter has had an abortion. Now all she does is cry. What can
I say that will help?

A young woman who has had an abortion will very likely live under a tremendous burden of guilt. What she needs is comfort, empathy, and, most importantly, a message of forgiveness. What she doesn't need is someone telling her about a woman's right to choose.

That's why we recommend that you take her to a crisis pregnancy center for counseling instead of a women's health clinic. We have seen firsthand the compassion and sensitivity that crisis pregnancy centers communicate to young girls who are broken over this decision. Many times these girls feel betrayed. Sometimes they were forced into a decision they weren't sure about. They were given no knowledge of what would happen to them emotionally. And now they're left with empty arms, trampled dreams, and paralyzing guilt, while everyone else has gone back to life.

Whatever you do, just be sure to be there for your daughter. This event has changed her life forever. If she ever needed you before, she needs you now.

DRUGS AND ALCOHOL

By the time my child was eight, he'd been confronted with drugs, guns, sex, pornography, theft, alcohol, and homosexuality. Do you think this is why he struggles so much as a teenager?

The things children are assaulted by today are unbelievable. They're introduced to hard-core vices at ever earlier ages. James Dean's bad boy character in *Rebel without a Cause* defied authority by racing jalopies and smoking. That same kid today has been a drug dealer for five years, has had multiple sexual encounters with multiple partners, has made crack addicts of every preteen he knows, and has shot at someone in anger.

Kids just aren't ready to deal with these things. They don't even know long division, but they have to know how to say no to free crack samples. They're having to grow up way too fast, and parents must give them the skills they need to cope or they risk losing them.

Your best ally in your battle to protect your child is a community of like-minded families. A moral community, coupled with a strong family identity at home, is the magic bullet, the secret pill that can both decrease the amount of temptation assaulting your child and help regulate him when he's not with you.

We don't mean you should isolate your family or your child from society, but that you should provide a safe community that is shielded from certain destructive forces. If you surround yourself with families who hold to the same ideals you do, you provide an environment of protection that can insulate your child from the terrible things he might otherwise have to deal with.

My teenager is a good kid. I don't have to worry about drugs or alcohol, do I?

This sounds like a naive question, but believe it or not, there are some parents who can say with confidence and accuracy, "My kids would never get involved in drugs or alcohol, certainly not on a long-term basis." These parents aren't "lucky," they've worked hard to be able to say this.

You may have done a wonderful job in raising your son or daughter, but every parent should still be wary. It doesn't take much to become physiologically addicted. Without the support of a moral community and in the presence of overwhelming peer pressure, even good kids can make wrong choices.

We live in a society that is consumed with the quick fix, the immediate high. Drug use has been glorified by music, television, and movies. It's got its own subculture, dress, and language. Someone looking for an identity different from the one he has could find it in this drug culture, especially if it offends Mom and Dad.

When your child goes to college or moves out of your home, you will not be there to monitor his behavior. So, even if you know your teen hasn't experimented with drugs or alcohol, before he leaves your home, you need to sit down and have an earnest discussion about it. "Honey, what's going to happen when you go off to college and some of the guys in the dorm say, 'Hey, why don't you just try this? It's really not so bad'?"

If a teenager hasn't had some dialogue beforehand, no matter how moral he is, he's *human*. "What would it hurt just to try it once?" So many times it's the good kid who ends up getting hooked because he didn't have any defenses in place.

Why not have this talk with your teen today?

I'm thinking that my teenager should try a little of everything, just to see what it's all about. That way it's easier to know if something should be accepted or rejected. Is this a good plan?

The idea that teenagers should try everything is a fallacy. Should they really try drugs to know that drugs are bad? How much experimentation with pornography do you want your son to do before he realizes it could be addictive? How much experimentation do you want your daughter to do with sexual activity before she realizes this is not right for her or for her body, or before she gets pregnant?

We like the story of the father whose children pleaded with him for permission to see a certain movie. It had their favorite actors, there was only a little sex in it, and the violence wasn't as bad as a lot of other movies. Besides, everyone else was seeing it. The father said no and remained firm. Then he went into the kitchen.

An hour or so later he offered his children some hot brownies. He'd used all their favorite ingredients, he explained: chocolate and eggs and flour and sugar. The children were reaching for brownies when he explained that in making them he'd mixed in only a tiny bit of dog poop. There wasn't as much in them as there could be, and they probably wouldn't taste it at all. Besides everybody else was eating brownies just like these.

Teenagers don't have to taste something to know it's not good for them. Parents are supposed to advise their children. They are there to teach them that certain things can hurt them. If you saw a mother letting her toddler play unattended by the freeway, you'd say that mother was irresponsible. Would it change your opinion if she explained she was doing it so he could find out for himself that playing by the freeway is dangerous?

Use your position as parent to save your teens from mistakes you could have kept them from.

REBELLION

I didn't discover your books until too late. My teenager is in complete rebellion. I'm so afraid and angry and hurt. What can I do?

There is a false notion in our society that, at age eighteen, your kids will cease to be your children and you can no longer influence them. Chances are, you're going to live the next twenty, thirty, even forty years on this earth, so you'll have decades with your adult children. You may have not had the best years with your children in the past, but you've got the rest of your life to make it right.

Begin by evaluating your own parenting to be sure you're not contributing to the problem. Then start working on rebuilding trust and influence. You haven't found this book too late. As long as you and your children both live, it's never too late to rebuild your relationship. Go back to chapter 1, and start rereading this book.

My teenager won't even talk to me. How can I work on the great communication suggestions you make in this book?

If you can't stand to look at each other because you know you're going to break out into a fight, then why not just slip a note under her door? It doesn't have to be a long note, and it certainly shouldn't be accusatory. Write something as simple as, "I really do love you. I'm just struggling, and I know you're struggling, too." And don't be surprised when a note comes flying by you when you've got your hands in the dishwater.

Sometimes we communicate better when we're not face-to-face. We can become so antagonistic to each other as parents and teens. Our physical presence reminds us of a hurtful word or a hurtful action, and before we know it, we're screaming. These walls can be broken down with just a simple note.

We would also recommend that you go back and reread the chapter on love languages. If you learn to express your love in ways your teen can understand and you persevere in doing so, eventually you will win through. Sometimes just placing your hand on your teenager's shoulder and saying, "I really appreciate what you've done," can break down a wall.

My teenager is showing signs that he doesn't respect me anymore. What can I do to regain my authority?

Usually the lack of respect for a parent has been there all along; it's just that the way a teenager demonstrates disrespect is more visible, especially now that the teenager is the same size or bigger than the parent. Sometimes a teen feels a greater sense of security in himself, like maybe he doesn't need to give respect to the parent anymore. In all probability, respect has been missing for a long time.

As we wrote in chapter 5, your goal shouldn't be to regain dominance over your teenager but to achieve influence. It's natural to want to control something that's out of control, especially when that something is your child. But when you have teenagers, using force won't get you where you want to go. You have no good options besides working to lead by your relational influence.

One area you'll want to work on is freedom. Not the unrestrained, do-whatever-you-want type of freedom, but the kind of freedom in which your teen is emancipated to communicate and to be his own person without the fear that an authority figure is going to force him to become something other than what he is.

It is also possible that you have misinterpreted your teen. What you are hopefully headed toward with your teenager is a peer relationship. But neither you nor your teen knows exactly how to act as equals. What you've interpreted as a lack of respect might be your teenager's first attempt at friendly familiarity. She might be teasing you.

It's usually quite clear when a teenager means to show disrespect. So, if you're not sure, and if your child usually doesn't speak this way, you might at least ask yourself whether you two are just reaching a point in your relationship where you feel you can have a little bit of fun.

Don't try to regain control. Work instead on regaining your teen's respect and trust. Sections 2 and 3 should give you some good ideas.

My teenager doesn't openly defy me but rather pushes the limit a bit. If I say be home by ten, she's home at ten-fifteen. Do I have grounds to be upset?

Assuming this happens regularly and without good reason, this is what we call microrebellion. When your child was four and you told her to stay on the carpet, did she stand with her foot on the carpet but her toes poking over onto the tile? When she was ten and you asked her to put her dirty clothes in the hamper, did she toss them *near* the hamper?

As we say in *On Becoming Preteen Wise,* for this young person microrebellion is full-scale rebellion. Parents may tend to dismiss this kind of rule bending as minor, but it is not minor to the child. Her toe may only be partly over the line, but her heart is completely over. Rebellion of any size, uncorrected, leads to contempt for authority. A microrebellious child who has not been corrected in the early or middle years is going to reveal the true depths of her rebellion as a teenager.

It's also possible for parents to unintentionally raise up a child who does not respect their instructions. When your son was five, how many times did you ask him to pick up his toys? If he delayed picking them up or did not pick them up all the time, did you finally do it for him? When he was nine, now many times did you have to ask him to put his bike in the garage before he finally did it? Did you nag? Did you threaten punishment but never follow through? If so, is it any wonder that your teenager doesn't think he needs to do what you ask?

Correct this problem by following our suggestions for how to regain influence with your teenager. Eventually you will want to confront your teen about his microrebellion. But be sure not to do it in the heat of the moment. When he strolls in at ten-fifteen is not the time. But you might want to talk about it tomorrow morning over cereal and coffee.

While the time for authoritative parenting is over with this child, it's never too late to mean what you say. If you set a curfew for your teenager, there has to be a consequence for breaking it. Otherwise, it's not a rule; it's a suggestion. It's time to grow a backbone, Mom or Dad. If your teen breaks the curfew without a good reason, enforce the consequence. A parent who does not follow through on promises will be despised.

There is something better than a curfew: trust. When the relationship between parents and teens is very good, certain rules become superfluous. The Ezzos set no curfew for their daughters. Because the girls had proven themselves trustworthy in the small things, their parents were willing to trust them in this.

But it wasn't a blind trust. It was a courtesy trust. It had parameters on it. The girls would tell their parents what their plans were and when they expected to be home. If those plans changed, they called home. But even in those conversations there was a mutual respect. It wasn't, "Hey, Mom and Dad, this is what we're going to do, so deal with it." It was a dialogue.

My teenager came home with a certain part of his (or her) body pierced. What can I do?

Every generation comes out with new fads to shock old folks. It was shocking in the fifties to watch the Fab Four come over from England with long hair. It created a rage: Suddenly, long hair was in, and the good, Republican, short haircut was out. It also created an outrage: People were talking about it, preaching about it, writing editorials on it. Long hair was thought to herald the decline of the American ethical system. Now long hair is mostly out and short hair is in again.

In the seventies, young girls started to wear bracelets around their ankles. Originally, that was the symbol for a prostitute, so parents didn't want their daughters wearing anklets. In time, it became just a style option and no longer carried the connotation of prostitution. It became culturally acceptable. The same is true for men wearing earrings or ponytails. Once it was done for rebellion; then it passed into the mainstream and became just a fashion choice.

These days the rage is tattooing and body piercing: nose, lip, tongue, eyebrow, belly button, etc. There is a shock value here. Many times a young person will adopt this style to express rebellion or nonconformity. Eventually, tattoos and body piercing will pass into the mainstream. Young people will get things painted or pierced simply because they truly believe it looks good. Some would argue that this transition has already taken place. Indeed, we know several delightful teenagers who have had their belly buttons pierced.

We think health concerns justify some limitations on body piercing. For instance, tongue piercing is out: You can't eat, and there's a danger of infection. If your teenager is considering body art or piercing, another thing you may want to discuss is the very real possibility that this style may go out of fashion. What may be considered attractive in ten years is a body that doesn't have pierce holes all over it. "Honey, just think about this: You might meet someone in a few years whom you'd dearly love to marry but who is totally turned off by the fact that you once had your nose pierced."

The question you have to ask when your teenager comes home with some body part pierced is why she did it. Was it done to offend authority or flout the establishment? Or did she do it just because her friend Julie did it, and it's the latest style? If her motive is to keep up with teen fads, that's one thing. But if she's done it out of insolence, the matter is more serious.

The teenager who comes home with something pierced in order to shock you is saying, "Hello, where have you been?" The pierced tongue, lip, nose, or eyebrow is your teen's way of telling you there is a disparity between who he is and who you are. When you see it, your tendency will be to give a knee-jerk reaction. "What in the world have you done!" That may, in fact, be the teen's goal: to at least get you to pay attention to him. You do need to deal with it, but we would advise you wait until you're cooled down.

When your teen does something like this to show he or she is rejecting you and your values, your inclination may be to strike back: "How can I hurt you for hurting me?" But that won't get you anywhere. Your teen is crying out to you that something is wrong, and he wants you to fix it. Otherwise why would you be the target of his shocking fashion statement? Just as suicide is so often a cry for help, so something like this is often a cry for attention.

Your question has to be, "How do I win him back?" That's going to be hard. The process will probably take months. You've got to regain the love, confidence, and trust of your teen. This gets back to the whole premise of this book, which is that you're going to fix most teen problems through the strength of your parent/teen relationship.

DISCIPLINE AND CONTROL

My teenager gets angry when I ask him (or her) to do chores around the house. What can I do to feel like I'm still in charge in this home? (Am I still in charge?)

First, evaluate what you are doing. Sometimes moms and dads, out of love and pure hearts, can find themselves doing everything for their children. Do you still clean up the dishes for them at dinnertime? Are you still pushing his chair in when he gets up from the table? Are you still making his bed and picking up his socks? Teens won't typically take ownership responsibility of behaviors if someone is always there reinforcing noncompliance. You may have to break yourself of certain habits before you'll be able to instill new, healthy habits into your children.

In chapter 6 we talked about responsibilities being monkeys.

Your children's monkeys love to jump back onto your shoulders. Your job is to instill in your child the responsibility of doing the chore himself. If you don't use the monkey repellant we discuss, you'll quickly be weighed down by countless chimps. We would encourage you to refer to that chapter.

A teen's refusal to do simple chores may be a symptom of a more serious problem than habit. You may just want to go back to the beginning and reread this entire book.

When he's with me, my teenager is well behaved. It's when he's not with me that worries me. How can I be sure he's acting properly when I'm not around?

Do you have just cause to believe your teenager is behaving poorly when apart from you? Are neighbors and school officials and other parents coming to you with similar negative reports about your teen? If you're getting a series of reports that are alarming to you, then do not let your teen's good behavior in your presence prevent you from exploring what is going on in his or her life.

Any of us is capable of making wrong choices from time to time. What you should be searching for is whether or not your teenager is characterized by this kind of misbehavior. Are you dealing with someone who acts out once every three years or once every three hours?

We should always think the best about our children. If your teenager feels you're waiting around the corner for him to fall so you can accuse him, you're not going to do anyone any favors. We should be expecting them to do the right thing. Your teen should feel you're counting on his good behavior, not waiting for misbehavior.

If it becomes clear that your teenager is behaving improperly when not in your presence, then you've got a high hill to climb. This goes back to what we said about not being able to leave your child at home alone. Until you can be certain of his behavior and until the bad reports stop coming in, you may not be able to leave him alone for extended periods.

But as you work through the principles in this book and your relationship with your teen sweetens, you may find this problem taking care of itself.

When I try to discipline my teen, he just gets into his car and drives off.

It could paralyze you to think that if you said something your teen didn't like, he might get into his car and flee. He could drive around the block, or he could take off across the country and you'd never know. On the other hand, if you allow this behavior to scare you into silence, your teen's temper tantrum has been successful.

There's not much you can do in the moment. You're not going to look your six-foot-two teenager in the eye and say, "You bend down, young man; I'm going to give you a spanking." If he drives off, he drives off. Just pray that he is safe until you have the opportunity to talk again.

In the meantime, go back to the beginning of this book and start applying some of the basic relational principles we've talked about. Start enhancing your marriage. Sit on the couch with your spouse and talk. Learn your teen's temperament. Learn yours. When he comes home, have a heart-to-heart talk, and continue these regularly as you move forward.

If you are making the payments on this car and if you are paying the insurance, it's appropriate for you to make decisions on how it's used and who uses it. Consider taking the keys away for a while.

While you're both sitting around the house wondering what to do, go for a walk together. Have a meaningful conversation over a meal or dessert. What America's teens are missing are moms and dads who take the time to talk with them. Parents work in hopes of giving their kids a great financial future. But you don't need to do that. Your kids will make a future for themselves if you give yourself over to them right now.

VIOLENCE AND CRIME

Although I can't prove it, I suspect my teenager has broken the law, perhaps more than once. I don't want to turn my own child in to the police. What should I do?

This situation might be best handled not by direct accusation but through a parable investigation. Use the Nathan parable as your model to set up a story that captures the essence of what you suspect your teen of doing (see chapter 6).

Let's say you suspect your son has been shoplifting. Perhaps you could design a hypothetical story about what happened at work today. "Son, I work with Mr. So-and-So. Just before five, I saw him take some pencils and pads of paper from the supply closet. I know he didn't take them to use them at work because I saw him get into his car with them and drive away. I think he's taking them home to his kids. I'm wondering about the rightness or wrongness of this. Son, tell me, what should I say to this man?"

Then, when he says it's definitely stealing, you can start bringing it around to the *you are the man* side. "So, it's wrong for someone to take things that don't belong to him and bring them home
for personal use?" Eventually, your teen may realize what you're
saying. That's when you should address the issue of what should be
done: "Okay, so what should this person do now to make it right?"

*Ever since my husband and I got divorced, our teenager has been
acting out violently. How can I help if reconciliation is not an option?*

Divorce will affect children differently according to a number of
variables, such as their age, personality, temperament, birth order,
which parent is leaving, and the longevity of the problem.

Consider the temperament of your teen. If he is very quiet and
internalizes everything, that's how he will handle the divorce. He
might become extremely sensitive, going into a tailspin at the
slightest provocation. On the other hand, a teenager who is vocal
and demonstrative about his emotions is going to be that way about
the divorce. He may begin responding violently. Sometimes this
will explode suddenly and then be over; other times it will be a
continued pattern of destructiveness—to himself, others, or both.

Another factor is the longevity of the problem. If it's been going
on a long time, there will be a root of bitterness there, an endless
wellspring of negative outpourings. A child who has been aware of
his parents' problems building for years, all the time wondering if
his world is going to hold together and finally seeing that it isn't,
might erupt into violence.

If your teen is acting out violently, we suggest the following six
ideas. First, in quiet moments, help her work through the grieving

stages that a child will go through with any great loss. Divorce is a loss: a loss of familiarity, a loss of a parent, a loss of an imagined future. There will be anger, denial, bargaining, and the rest. Divorced parents have to deal with grief, too, so why not work through it together?

Second, provide stability. Your teenager's universe has just come unglued. That's enough change for anyone to handle. Don't change everything else in the process. If it's at all possible, stay in the same house, and let your child keep his own friends and stay in his own school. Keep familiarity around wherever you can. Let as many things as possible remain fixed.

Third, listen to your teen. If you never had talk times before, now's the time to start having them. If you've had them all along, have twice as many now. If your teen feels she's not being heard or if you are closing her out, too, she may resort to more destructive means to get your attention. Your teenager needs you to have time for her.

Fourth, be around stable families, families in which there is both a husband and a wife at home. Encourage your teen to visit friends who come from stable homes. It's not that single-parent families are to be avoided, but simply that problems sometimes propagate problems. Sometimes things rub off onto your teen from the families he's around. Try to be sure what rubs off will be healthy things from stable families.

Fifth, provide an atmosphere of forgiveness. If every time you speak with your teen you're talking about your lousy ex, you'll be feeding him anger and frustration. He probably still has a child's devotion to that parent even though he knows some of what's happened. Your accusations mount up against his loyalty and create a riptide in his heart. No wonder he's acting out. You need to work through your own anger (leaving your children out of it) and arrive at forgiveness. Then begin encouraging your teen to forgive, too. She will need to forgive the other parent, you, and most likely herself.

Sixth, find someone to lean on. Get good counsel from someone you trust. Find someone for your teen to lean on, too. If there is a stable same-gender family member or friend who can be there for the child, make arrangements for that to happen on a regular basis. You're not trying to replace the parent who has left, but just to give your teen even a few crumbs of Daddy or Mommy time.

Even if you do all this, some kids just won't be able to handle it. Some will act out violently, others will get into drugs, commit crimes, and get pregnant (or impregnate). If that happens, tell your teen that if he's going to go overboard, that's his choice. But that you will be there for him when he comes back around and needs you.

As we have maintained throughout our books, the best situation for a child is to have a father and a mother who love each other and are committed to the family. Any other state of affairs is less than ideal and places serious obstacles in a child's path to healthy adulthood. But if divorce does come, use these suggestions to lessen the pain.

My teenager has mentioned suicide a few times. Should I take it seriously?

You should definitely take it seriously anytime a young person makes a threat to himself or others. Especially since suicide has been so glorified by the media. People think this will be their way to have their day in the sun. The problem is that the one who commits suicide never knows whether or not he had his day.

These are the types of things that you may want to mention to your teen's teacher, your clergy, or a school counselor to get advice and verification. You also need to get educated. Counselors have a whole checklist of behaviors to watch for. This will help you identify the potential warning signs of a teenager who is suicidal. Start being observant. Is your child becoming more isolated, cutting off ties, being removed from friends, becoming more moody, locking himself into his room?

Do not take a chance. The best thing that could happen is for you to find out that your teen was just talking about suicide to get your attention. If so, evaluate how you might be able to devote more talk time to the relationship. It would be a tragedy if you ignored legitimate warning signs. When someone mentions suicide, she is usually crying out, "Would you look at me? Would you help me?" It's not always that she really wants to end her life, but that she's just asking for someone to come to her aid. If you were not to respond to these cries, that could be the straw that breaks the camel's back.

Take suicide talk seriously.

My twelve-year-old son has drugged me numerous times and tried to kill me. I'm not kidding. I can't live like this anymore. Help! He also leaves the pool gate open purposely, hoping to encourage our three-year-old daughter to go for a swim at the bottom of the pool. He has admitted his motives. I've worked through Preteen Wise *and a host of other books and courses. What can I do short of having him arrested and taken from our home?*

If you have a situation like this, you should immediately call social services to get a referral. Having your child arrested is probably not necessary at this point, but having him evaluated definitely is. Call your local mental health center. Talk to your clergy. Find out where you can get help. You are dealing with seriously destructive, disturbed behavior that needs immediate attention.

It's sad to say, but sometimes the best option is to have a child like this removed from the home for a while, especially if you fear for the safety of other children or yourself. An organization like Teen Challenge may be ideal to handle this situation.

You'll want to do some careful soul searching here. Children don't usually develop this kind of behavior by themselves. Often in cases like this, one or both parents are out of control. It may not only be the child who needs professional help.

THE MEDIA

I'm so fed up with my teenager's media choices that I'm just about ready to cancel cable, throw away the TV and the radio, break some CDs, and sell our computer. Before I go on my rampage, is there a better way to react?

When parents who now have teenagers began their parenting in the mid-1980s, they did not have the media pressure that is in force today. Back then, all we had in our homes were TVs and stereos. Now we've got multiple computers, all hooked to the Internet, VCRs and DVDs, big-screen TVs with surround sound THX speakers, console video games, palmtops, CD boom boxes, and remote controls by the dozen.

Who would have guessed that communications technology would advance so quickly? It's understandable that parents may feel they're coming late to the media game. However, that's where we are, and there's no going back. Your teenager may have many more ways to offend you with his media choices today, but in the end it's no different from the teen who shocked his parents by listening to rock 'n' roll on the radio in the fifties.

Is this your home? Are you still paying the mortgage? Are you still covering the insurance costs? Do you still put food on the table? Are there certain things that are offensive to you? Here again, parents, you need to get a backbone. You have a right to influence what your kids watch while they're in your house. Don't be afraid to apply some pressure to limit things that create destructive attitudes or patterns of behavior. You need to encourage some self-control and set some limitations.

When you do, it's very possible that your kids will welcome your restrictions. Every child grows in respect for parents who know how to take a stand at the right time, at the right place, in the right way.

Also read our section in chapter 3 on the part media plays in teen rebellion.

My teenager plays video games from the moment he gets home from school until I force him to go to bed at night. I'm thinking things are a little out of control. Am I crazy, or could he be addicted to that thing?

Yes, it's very possible that this could be an addiction of sorts, especially if the teen has an obsessive kind of personality. The good news is that there is no physiological, chemical addiction involved.

If video games (or computer games or Internet time) have gotten out of control in your teen's life, especially if it's begun to impact other areas of behavior, it's time for you to intervene. Take away the privilege for a while. Work to help him regain his balance and redraw his priorities.

It's good for you and your teen both to know that certain things could become problems in the future. Awareness of the propensity should help you instill defenses against future addictive temptations when they come. There are good resources for computer and Internet addiction in books and on the Web.

SPIRITUALITY

My daughter has gotten into Wicca. Is this just pretend, more like a girl's club than anything serious, or should I be concerned?

You should be very concerned. One regrettable development in the last generation has been the rise in interest in witchcraft and the occult, especially among teenage girls. Twenty-plus years ago, witchcraft wasn't a real concern in America. Kids dressed up as witches on Halloween, bearing their brooms and black hats from doorbell to doorbell. Today witchcraft and occult activities are very real and can go as far as animal sacrifice, torture, and ritual prostitution.

Because of its worship of its mother goddess, witchcraft can seem appealing to teenage girls. Those who hold feminist ideals can find the ideologies compatible. Young girls can feel out of control in their lives, so no wonder a system that offers spells and potions to bend things to one's will would interest them.

Covens are filled mostly with girls. They are ruled by high priestesses. Their rituals celebrate the mystery of womanhood under the light of the moon, to whose cycle all women are connected. Add to this the thrill of deviancy associated with the occult, and you've got a clear picture of what can make Wicca alluring to teenage girls.

If you suspect your daughter is experimenting with the occult, you need to get educated. Go online or get to your public library. Your clergy may be helpful here. Wiccan rituals can involve chants and spells, astral projection, drugs, so called "blood control" (which involves binding parts of the body with cords), scourging, and ritual sex, not to mention animal and even human sacrifice. What may seem harmless to you and what your daughter may promise you is harmless may in fact be deadly.

We are no longer talking about the kindergarten black hat, black cat kind of witchcraft we used to see on Bugs Bunny cartoons. We're talking about a spiritual darkness that is very real and that preys upon the innocent, promising glory but bringing doom.

My teenager has begun hearing voices and acting strangely, sometimes like someone else entirely. Is this just hormones, or should I be concerned? Should I see somebody about this? If so, who?

Yes, you need to get your teen to someone right away. Whom you choose and how you interpret this behavior are up to you. You may go straight to a psychiatrist and get some tranquilizers, or you may go to your clergy and come at this from a spiritual direction. You may do both and more besides. Just get help.

I don't want to impose my own beliefs or values on my teenager. I want him to find his own spiritual path. How can I help with that?

Let us ask you this: Why are your beliefs insufficient? Do you really mean that the beliefs you've built your life on aren't worth passing on to your children? If you have virtue in your life, don't you want to pass that on? If you've learned hard lessons in your life, wouldn't you want to spare your child that pain?

This goes back to the question of whether teenagers should try a little of everything just to see what's good and what's bad. We don't think that's wise. One of the main reasons parents are around is to teach their children the lessons they've learned so their children don't have to learn it the hard way. It's the same with your beliefs and values. These are at the core of your being—even if you don't think you're a spiritual person. We all have foundational beliefs that govern everything we do.

If you're certain your solutions are right, why not equip your children with what works? If you think your beliefs are wrong, then maybe you need to get some new beliefs. But even if you're on a journey of spiritual discovery yourself, there are still some baseline beliefs that advise you. Don't leave your teenager in spiritual darkness, especially if you have found the light.

If your teenager doesn't stand for something, he's likely to fall for anything.

My teenager says she's become a Buddhist. Does a parent have any say over that sort of thing?

First, assess what your teenager is actually saying. Is she really convinced that the Four Noble Truths are the path to enlightenment, or is this just the equivalent of a nose ring? Has she arrived at the feet of Buddha after deep soul searching, or is this simply the religion du jour among the in group?

If you conclude that this is merely a stunt to get your attention, then treat it that way. Focus on your relationship. Sit down and talk. Find out where she's hurting or where she's feeling a lack. Find out what she's hoping Buddhism will give her that she's not getting now. Increase your talk time and, if possible, Daddy time. If the need that caused this announcement gets met in the family, she may decide Buddha's not for her after all.

There is a saying, attributed to Blaise Pascal, which asserts that man has in his heart a God-shaped void. The religious impulse is attested in every age and every culture. There does seem to be in man both a need and a natural propensity to believe in a supernatural power or being. That your teenager is beginning to explore her spirituality is as natural as eating and sleeping. It is part of mankind's universal search for meaning and inner peace.

If you have not held to religious beliefs as you raised your child, his choice of Buddhism (or Islam or Christianity or whatever) may be because he has genuinely found something that resonates with his spirit. On the other hand, if you have raised your child to hold to one religious system and he chooses one that is different or even opposed to it, that's saying something else entirely. It may be that he has truly found something in his new faith—or he may just be rebelling against you.

If you have been nominal in your beliefs, your teen may be rebelling against your hypocrisy and searching for substance. She may be longing for something worth living for, something or someone beyond herself worth committing to.

We, the authors of *Teenwise,* know that man has a longing to know the one true God. We believe that God has spoken; He is personal; and He provides all the spiritual resources for life. We believe He has revealed Himself in His Son, Jesus Christ, and that through Him anyone can be reconciled to God, purified from the inside out, and live with Him eternally.

We would invite the reader to look into true Christianit for yourself and your family. God has promised in the Bible that if you seek Him with all your heart, you will find Him (Jeremiah 29:13).

Letting Go

a s we come to the end of our book, it is fitting to talk about letting your teenager go. One day, for better or worse, he will rise up out of the nest and fly under his own power. It's not the end. You'll be seeing him regularly for the rest of your life. But it will be the end of a phase. For eighteen years or so you've tended to his needs, listened to his hurts, challenged and corrected him, and simply been there for him.

Our hope is that this is a happy time for you, a time for you and your grown child to enter the friendship stage of parenting. One day soon he may find a mate and begin a family of his own. You are no longer in a position of authority over him, but he will hopefully seek your counsel. And you will always have your common moral foundation binding you together.

What exactly does it mean to let go of your child? The most important thing to understand is that it is an ongoing process. It begins when your child is very young. The day the Ezzos' eldest daughter, Amy, took her first steps, Gary and Anne Marie had to let go of her little hand and allow her the freedom to walk on her own. From that moment on the process repeated itself many times. Gary remembers the day he and Anne Marie waved good-bye to her on her first day of school. Years later they watched as she drove away in the car for the first time by herself.

Day by day we let go of our babies, young children, teens, and young adults. Hopefully you've been equipping your child for this moment all along, instilling in him the ability to handle adult life. You've done this by teaching him to be responsible for his own actions, helping him internalize a moral code, and giving him basic survival skills such as a work ethic and the ability to balance a checkbook.

Your whole parenting career has been in preparation for this moment. Consequently, it is natural for parents to hesitate at the threshold, wondering what will come next.

THE EMOTIONS OF LETTING GO

Two emotions conflict when in the process of letting go: fear and confidence. The two are related. In its purest form, fear is untested confidence.

Throughout the child-rearing process, parents live with the fear of letting go—until confidence replaces it. During her crawling stage, Jennifer Ezzo stayed in her playpen while Anne Marie did work around the house. But as Jennifer grew older and learned the boundaries her parents had established for the living room, they relaxed their tight supervision and gave her more freedom. Notice that this happened only when their confidence in Jennifer's ability to play safely in the living room had replaced their fear that she might hurt herself.

Note that she was not suddenly granted total freedom. She wasn't yet free to go outside and play in the neighbor's yard. As she earned her parents' confidence, they expanded her freedoms. But there was a gradual, logical progression at work.

Maybe you didn't realize it, but you've been letting go all along. Each step in the growth of your child has probably seen fear being replaced with confidence. In area after area, parental control gave way to freedom. As he demonstrated responsible behavior within your defined limits, you expanded his boundaries. Guess what? Expanding boundaries to allow greater freedom is the very process of letting go.

WHAT AM I ULTIMATELY LETTING GO OF?

You never let go of your children. Not really. They will always be your children. Nor do you let go of your influence. Ultimately, you are only letting go of one thing: exercising authority over them.

As your child grows, you're continually giving up your right to rule over them, make decisions for them, and control their environment. You're exchanging the exercise of your authority for the confidence that you have trained them to be responsible for making right decisions in their lives. As they grow older and become more trustworthy, you continue to yield up more of your rights over them.

This can be a fearful thing for some parents, especially the permissive parent who let go of too much too early or the authoritarian parent who could never let go at all. With both parenting styles, trust in the relationship is absent, making letting go impossible. We're hoping that's not the case with you. You're hopefully enjoying a trust not only in what you have done with your children through your parenting skills, but also a mutual trust *with* your children.

It is this trust that makes letting go possible. You have reached the pinnacle of your parenting. Relax and enjoy it. Your mature trust in each other will bind you closer than ever before.

HEADED HOME

We began this journey with a story about a couple who had gotten so lost they weren't even on the surface of the earth anymore. Parents of teenagers can feel that way, can't they? We've spent these pages trying to give you a plan for not only getting back to earth but for heading toward your most desired splashdown point. You may wish you'd never taken the wrong turns in the first place, but at least now you're headed home.

Parenting is never without regrets, even for the healthiest family. We all wish for the opportunity to hit the reset button and go reclaim those moments when we were out of control or missed a precious opportunity. There were times in all our lives when we didn't know which way to turn. We often make ourselves half crazy trying to decide exactly what to do about the teen in our home. But we cannot begin to change the status quo without accepting responsibility for change.

What things are you changing? For some, change means adopting a whole new set of values. But for most of us it is not a change in values that is needed but rededication to the ones we already have.

Either way, you begin with the starter kit of basic values. Included are honesty, kindness, loyalty, forgiveness, and respect for one another. Honesty is a must, and it goes two ways. You expect it from your teens, and you need to give it to them as well. Being believable and trustworthy are synonymous with being honest.

Kindness is not old-fashioned; it's necessary.

In the rebuilding process, this virtue must assuredly be applied to our speech. We must practice the counsel of the old proverb, "A soft answer turns away wrath, but a harsh word stirs up anger." Loyalty means that we're not going to hang out our dirty laundry for everyone else to see. We'll deal with our problems inside the home where the process of loving and protecting each other begins. Without forgiveness, relationships cannot go forward, for forgiveness is a prerequisite to restoration. And without restoration you abide in a continuing state of war.

Respect for each other starts with the fifth commandment, "Honor your father and mother that your days may be long upon the land which the Lord your God is giving you." To teens we say, "Honor your parents, for God used them to give you life. They participated in the creation process. You live because of them." To parents we say, "Your children were born bearing the image of God. Your teen possesses human dignity. Respect his dignity, for anything less is tantamount to disrespect for God."

Becoming a healthy family is learning to turn to God with our needs, and turn to Him diligently, perhaps on our knees. He listens to us, cares about our concern, and knows our hurts. Restoring and rebuilding relationships takes time and spiritual energy.

Raising teenagers can be a wearying task at times. It's understandable that we may want to throw our hands up when confronted by difficulties with our kids, do nothing, and hope for the best. But as adults we can't do that because we know God won't do that with us. Remember, you will have your children for a lifetime, not just for a season. Love and enjoy them.

Index

MORE WISDOM FOR PARENTS

Over One Million Babywise Parents!

ON BECOMING BABYWISE I
(ages 0-12 months)

A great book for parents who would like to enjoy quiet nights filled with peaceful sleep. Covers such topics as feeding philosophies, hunger and sleep cycles, and establishing the baby's routine.
ISBN 0-9714532-0-9

ON BECOMING CHILDWISE
(ages 3-7 years)

Learn how to avoid common problems that may lie ahead in your child's teen years. A must-read for parents who want to help their children make a healthy transition into adolescence.
ISBN 0-9714532-3-3

ON BECOMING BABYWISE II
(ages 5-15 months)

Babywise II teaches parents how to instill in their pretoddlers right learning patterns that will help them successfully manage instructions, directions, freedoms, limitations, and relationships as they grow.
ISBN 0-9714532-1-7

ON BECOMING PRETEEN WI
(ages 8-12 years)

Gary Ezzo and Robert Bucknam, M.D. say "begin with the end in mind" wh parenting youth ages eight-to-twelve years-old. Prevent teenage rebellion when you practice these hands-on strategies for building a relationship with your child now!
ISBN 0-9714532-4-1